How to DRIF

The Art of
Oversteer

PAUL MORTON

S-A DESIGN

CarTech®

Edited By: Travis Thompson

ISBN 978-1-61325-013-6

CarTech®

39966 Grand Avenue
North Branch, MN 55056
Telephone (651) 277-1200 • (800) 551-4754 • Fax: (651) 277-1203
www.cartechbooks.com

OVERSEAS DISTRIBUTION BY:

Brooklands Books Ltd.
P.O. Box 146, Cobham, Surrey, KT11 1LG, England
Telephone 01932 865051 • Fax 01932 868803
www.brooklands-books.com

Brooklands Books Aus.
3/37-39 Green Street, Banksmeadow, NSW 2019, Australia
Telephone 2 9695 7055 • Fax 2 9695 7355

Front Cover:
Every generation strives to create something uniquely their own, and drifting is a completely new and fresh motorsport that will define the latest generation of automotive enthusiasts. Drifting competition isn't a rehash of on an old idea; it's an exciting and innovative new way to be creative with a car. This book is written by an enthusiast, for enthusiasts, as well as those who are just learning about drifting. It was written to explain the very misunderstood art of oversteer.

Title Page:
Though a drift car may look like it's being pushed beyond its limit, it's actually being driven under very precise control. A car that has actually been pushed beyond its control limit will either spin out or slide in a direction other than the driver had intended, very possibly crashing into something. As you have no doubt seen in drifting videos and live competition, drift drivers can consistently slide smoothly and precisely through a series of turns, directing their cars exactly where they want them to go—how would that be possible without control?

Back Cover, Top:
You can break down each turn of a drifting track into its turn-in, clipping, and exit points. Flip through Chapters 2 and 3 and check out the helpful diagrams used to illustrate high-performance driving and drifting techniques. (Rob Benner)

Middle:
Coil-overs are important because they allow you to adjust ride height and corner weights to help your car oversteer or otherwise tweak your handling for a specific course.

Bottom:
Drifting is more than just a TV or movie gimmick or the random act of sliding a car sideways—it's precision driving at its finest.

DEDICATION

Along with all the people who put up with me while I wrote this book, I would like to dedicate it to Steve Hendrickson—the guy who gave me the opportunity to do it.

ABOUT THE AUTHOR

Paul Morton has been enthusiastic about one thing or another for his entire life. Growing up in the 1970s he found himself immersed in the BMX culture. From there, it was on to skateboarding and eventually BMX freestyle. In the mid 1980s, he got his driver's license and his first car, which lead him into the minitruck and VW scenes. What really grabbed Paul's attention in the 1980s was the world of car stereo competition. This was a new and exciting way to be creative with a car. Mobile electronics would turn out to be his main focus well into the 1990s as he both competed in IASCA sound competitions and worked at various stereo shops as a custom mobile electronics installer. In 1995, Paul's hobby led into his first publishing job as the editor of Auto Sound & Security Magazine. This is where he stumbled upon yet another thing to be enthusiastic about—photography.

While Paul honed his skills as a photographer, writer, and magazine editor, a new genre was gaining momentum in the automotive aftermarket: the import scene. Around the turn of the millennia, a small publishing company decided to launch a title dedicated to this market and Paul found himself at Y-Visionary Publishing, where he became the first editor of *Import Racer!* Magazine. This was a publication dedicated to the tuner market and one of the first to offer extensive drifting coverage. Y-Visionary was also the first U.S. publishing company to create magazine specifically for this new motorsport, entitled *Drifting*—and Paul Morton was co-editor.

Paul is presently a freelance photographer and is responsible for the majority of the photographs in this book—unless it has specific photo credit, Paul shot it. For him, drifting is yet another way to be creative with a car. Since the first drifting events that came to the U.S., Paul has photographed, written about, and taken part in the sport and subculture of drifting.

PREFACE

Drifting is the most exciting thing you can do on four wheels. And although competitive drifting is new to us here in the U.S., we have been watching it on TV and in the movies for decades. Since the origin of the car chase, directors have employed the technique of sliding a car sideways around various corners to give the impression of speed and create a sense of urgency. Even before it had a name, drifters made it clear that they weren't slowing down for anything, not even the turns! Drifting may not be the fastest way around a corner, but in the movies and in real life, it certainly is the most exciting.

Today, the art of sliding a car sideways is more popular than ever. Even the general public can experience it in everything from video games to TV commercials. We owe this to the competitive sport of drifting, which has recently found its way from Japan to the U.S.

The art of drifting is extremely difficult to master and only drivers that possess exceptional car control skills can do it well consistently. Most people don't understand all that it takes to drift, whether they're seeing it on TV or in a drifting competition. Drifting requires accuracy, precision, control, and commitment. This book was written to shed some light on what is required for a car and its driver to drift, and hopefully it will shatter some of the myths and misconceptions surrounding this intriguing new motorsport.

This is the budget project 240SX that Paul built while putting together this book. See Chapters 5 and 6 to see how the car came together.

AN INTRODUCTION TO DRIFTING

Unlike racing, where elapsed time or a finish line determines the winner, drifting is judged on style and intensity. Judges use various criteria including the angle of attack, execution, style, speed, and amount of tire smoke to determine the winner. Skilled drivers like Chris Forsberg can consistently incorporate all of these elements into their drifting for a successful run that will earn maximum points.

On paper it's not even possible, but the art of drifting is real. Drifting is the newest, most exciting motorsport since the invention of the limited-slip differential—it may very well be the most exhilarating amalgamation of man and machine ever devised! From the winding mountain passes and desolate industrial roads of Japan, this unique sport of sliding a car sideways through a series of corners has made its way to America. Drift, or dorifto, as they call it Japan, extracts the most exciting element from various forms of auto racing, amplifies it, and makes it the focus of an extremely exhilarating new motorsport.

If you've watched cars race, you've seen them "drift" in every motorsport from touring and Formula One to sprint and rally. Today you can see drifting everywhere from movies to TV commercials, you can do it in video games, and it's quite possible that you have actually put your car into a drift yourself. Have you ever broken your rear tires loose in a corner and steered into the skid, or away from the turn to correct? If so, then you have performed the very essence of a drift. It's an exhilarating feeling to control a vehicle under this condition, and I'm just talking about the simple oversteer correction! Now imagine the same feeling, but much more exaggerated, on a twisted road course that resembles a winding mountain road. You attack corner after corner, at speed, tires smoking, pitching the car from one direction to the other, sliding sideways around each turn on the very edge of control. It's intense, it's exciting, and this is what the sport of drifting is all about.

Make no mistake about it—drifting is an art. It's arguably the most difficult motorsport to master and many people simply aren't able to do

Odds are you've already put your car into a drift—though probably not to this level. When rear tire traction is greatly reduced in a turn, whether intentionally or not, the rear end of the car will slide toward the outside of the turn. This is called oversteer. Turning into the slide and easing off the throttle will correct this condition and hopefully keep you from spinning out. In the sport of drifting, drivers oversteer intentionally and take it to the extreme by staying on the throttle and steering into the slide. They utilize the same car control techniques used in racing to keep the car from spinning.

Exhibition drifting is all about hanging the rear end out as far as possible and sliding the car sideways with maximum slip angle. What makes this so difficult is that the tires are being pushed to their limit of traction, and therefore the car is being driven at the very edge of control. Making one small mistake, like applying too much throttle, will reduce traction to the point that there isn't enough to keep the rear end from coming all the way around and the car from spinning out.

it. Those who can are considered some of the best drivers in the world due to their intimate knowledge of the driving techniques and car control skills necessary for drifting. Although reading this book won't make a drifter out of you (only a seemingly limitless amount of dedication and practice coupled with a certain amount of natural talent can do that), this is exactly where you need to start if you are serious about the sport. You'll learn the history and definition of drifting, the required driving techniques necessary to initiate, maintain, and exit a drift, and how to choose a drift car and set it up specifically for drifting. Ultimately, if you're serious about this sport, you'll want to find an organized drift event so you can experience the excitement for yourself—this book helps you with that as well.

What Exactly is Drifting?

Drifting, in its most basic form, has been around since the invention of the automobile, although the first people to do it most likely didn't drift intentionally. Drifting basically refers to an oversteer condition. You can think of oversteer as literally "steering too much." That is to say, the car turns more than steering input alone would allow it to. If you turn the steering wheel all the way to one side when driving relatively slowly, you'll simply drive around in tight circles. But enter a corner fast enough and try to steer your way through it without slowing down and you will lose traction and begin to slide. Assuming your car has a tendency to oversteer, the rear end will slide to the outside of the turn, rotating the car more than would be possible with just the steering input. This allows you to follow a tighter

Drifting often takes place on a winding road course. This sequence shows how a car must set up and drift around a corner, designated by cones in this case, and then Switchback to drift around the next corner in the opposite direction.

line or path through that turn. If you do this while continuing to steer into the turn, you will undoubtedly spin out. To correct an oversteer condition like this, you should countersteer (steer in the direction of the skid, away from the turn), which is also referred to as

opposite lock. If your intention is just to get through a corner without spinning out (by choice or not), you want to countersteer and let off the throttle just enough to regain traction. As this happens, gradually steer back into the corner and continue through it.

If you want to drift through a similar turn (whether you're at a drifting event or a race), you need to stay on the throttle and purposefully break your rear tires loose, with one or more of several techniques, once you've entered a corner at speed. If everything is going as planned, the rear end of the car will start to come around and slide through the turn. This is when you want to counter-steer, or turn your front wheels to opposite lock, so that you won't spin out. At the same time you have to maintain just the right amount of rear wheel spin to maintain the drift. As you slide around the corner, your car will lose some of its momentum and slow down enough so that the rear tires can regain sufficient traction and you will be able to straighten the front wheels and come out of the drift as you exit the corner. After all that, you have to set up the car to do it again in the next corner, typically in the opposite direction! The result of a well-executed drift is exhilarating for both the driver and spectators—but if you screw it up, you'll find yourself either in an understeer condition (the opposite of oversteer, when the front tires lose traction in a turn) or spinning out. Although it may sound simple, it's the fine line between maintaining and losing control that makes drifting so challenging and exciting.

Japanese Origins

If necessity is the mother of invention, then perhaps boredom is the father of hobbies. We all tend to find ways to amuse ourselves and pass time based upon what is right in front of us. It's no different from the first surfers who bolted roller-skate wheels to a board so they could surf on the sidewalk when waves weren't an option, or when early hot-rodders

stripped parts off readily available cars and modified their engines to see who could do it better and go faster. In Japan they have mountain roads—loads of them—and well-balanced, high-performance cars with extremely well engineered suspension systems. It was an adventurous group of people in the mid 1960s, dubbed the Rolling Zoku, which brought it all together. They attacked the winding mountain roads of Rokkosan, Hakone, Irohazaka, and Nagano with the sole intention of finding the quickest way between two points.

In the beginning these racers were into "gripping," and their goal was trimming precious seconds of their elapsed time, just like in any other form of racing. Skillful drivers learned to brake going into a corner and trim enough speed, and thus momentum, to traverse the corner and get back on the throttle to exit quickly—all the time maintaining as much traction as possible. As the skill level of the Rolling Zoku pro-

gressed, the drivers came closer to the handling limits of their vehicles and ultimately surpassed them. They found that by keeping on the throttle and breaking their rear wheels loose in a turn, and then steering into the skid to correct, they could drift through a corner with much less braking. This allowed them to maintain most of their momentum and keep engine RPM up. Thus, it was in the name of lower elapsed times that these drivers first studied and adapted various drifting techniques from rally racing to the often treacherous mountain passes.

Drivers found that this new technique didn't necessarily lower their elapsed times through the turns, but it was certainly the most fun way to get through them! Later on, Keiichi Tsuchiya, the man who many consider to be the father of modern professional drifting, would say: "I drift not because it is the quickest way around a corner, but because it is the most exciting way." Tsuchiya, host of the popular Japanese

Various elements of drifting were adapted from rally racing and then applied to driving on the street. You've probably also seen drifting in sprint car racing and even road racing to a lesser extent. (Ford Motor Company)

Keiichi "Dori Kin" or "Drift King" Tsuchiya is known as the father of modern day drifting. He is one of the people responsible for creating the D1 Grand Prix. An ex-street racer and now retired racecar driver, he still oversees the D1GP events and has judged every one held in the U.S.

television show Best Motoring, played a pivotal role in popularizing drifting as a motorsport. One of Tsuchiya's biggest influences was a driver named Kunimitsu Takahashi, a motorcycling legend turned racecar driver in the 1970s. Takahashi used a very aggressive style, regularly drifting as a racing technique. Captivated by Takahashi's techniques, Tsuchiya began using drift techniques on the streets, earning him a reputation among the Japanese street racing crowd. Tsuchiya later competed in several amateur racing events, using the aggressive drift techniques that eventually earned him the title "Drift King."

As popularity for this late-night, underground activity grew, drivers in the cities of Japan picked up the practices of the Touge drivers and applied the new techniques in their very own backyard. Touge (noun, not verb) is a Japanese word that literally translates to "pass," referring to a mountain pass or a narrow road with many turns. Urban drivers couldn't take advantage of the continuous mountain corners, but they did have vast industrial areas that were all but vacant at night. These industrial drifters began to add their own unique flavor to the driving and modified their cars to not only drift better, but also to appear outrageous to the hoards of spectators that gathered to witness their surreal driving skills.

Much like the illegal street races that have gone on in the United States for decades, drifting on public roads in Japan is illegal. However, over there, the local police do have a certain level of tolerance. Drifters are allowed to perform their art for a specific amount of time in the middle of the night. If the drifting goes on for too long, a police car will drive through with lights flashing and horns wailing. Typically, no citations are issued, and everyone just goes home. We cannot recommend testing the authorities in your area on this matter, as drifting and racing on public streets is both very dangerous and highly illegal.

Drifting Goes Legit

The next logical step for drifting was to do it at legal, organized events. Drifters who once honed their skills in the hills and on the desolate industrial roads of Japan under the shroud of night soon found themselves gathering during the day at racetracks to drift in a much safer, more controlled environment. With a safe consistent place to practice, skill levels steadily increased to the point where drifters

Although illegal, in Japan drifters frequent deserted industrial roads to hone their skills. This is how the early pioneers of the sport started out after word spread about the drifting that was going on in the winding mountain roads. To this day the tradition of drifting late into the night goes on and Japanese police are said to have a certain level of tolerance for it. (Scott Kanemura/Drifting Magazine)

wanted to find out who had the most skill—and thus, drifting competition was born! Early organized drift trials were originally just for fun. They grew into regional drift contests that were professionally judged, typically by other drifters, as the judges had to be intimately familiar with drifting style and technique. These events were known as Ikaten and were created by *Video-Option,* a monthly video magazine version of the ever-popular *Option* magazine. They took place in all the major cities of Japan along with the Driver's Search. Driver's Search was just that, a way to drum-up new talent for the Ikaten events, while also allowing enthusiasts a way to safely break into drifting without reverting to practicing on public roads.

As drifting popularity grew and skill levels progressed, Japanese performance parts manufacturers took notice and wanted to get in on the action. They began producing drift-specific parts to accommodate the fledgling sport that was growing before their eyes. Kei Office was one early Japanese company that stood out for its drifting and suspension wares. Its first name comes from Kei-

Japanese drifters eventually found their way to the track, where organized events were held to let drivers hone and showcase their skills. This gave them a much safer place to practice and elevate the sport of drifting to the next level, which they did. The increased skill level and the Japanese spectators' desire for drifting led to the D1 Grand Prix.

Daijiro Inada is not only the founder of Option *Magazine and* Option Video, *but also the infamous Tokyo Auto Salon. Now he can also take credit (and undoubtedly a load of cash) for being part of the team that created the D1GP, which brought drifting down from the hills of Japan and placed it prominently on the world's stage.*

ichi Tsuchiya, who still runs the company today. Autolink currently distributes Kei Office parts in the U.S. It was ultimately the vision of a magazine publisher that brought drifting into the mainstream and eventually onto the world stage. Daijiro Inada, who founded both the Tokyo Auto Salon and *Option* magazine, knew that drifting would have a huge following as a motorsport if he brought it up to a professional level. So in 2001, along with the help of his good friend and professional Touring Car driver Keiichi Tsuchiya, he created the D1 Grand Prix (D1GP). This is the pinnacle of drifting competition anywhere on the planet, with events in the U.S., Europe, Korea, and, of course, Japan. D1GP is an invaluable resource to the growth if drifting, as awareness and enthusiasm increase with every event.

In Japan, the D1GP drifting series is hugely popular and drifters are treated like celebrities. Drifting is a full-fledged sport and big business, with corporate sponsorships and loads of merchandise. Besides drift-

specific car parts, there are numerous drifting videos and various toys from diecast to R/C cars. There is even a manga series called *Initial D,* which was later adapted into a televised anime program. It features Takumi Fujiwara, a tofu delivery boy who drifts his father's AE86 Corolla through the hills of Japan, seemingly unaware of drifting's popularity among his fellow teens. Incidentally, Keiichi Tsuchiya has been an editorial supervisor on the televised anime *Initial D,* and even appeared in episode 23 (First Stage) as a special guest.

Drifting in the U.S.

Today, drifting in the U.S. is in its infancy and only recently has it grown to be accepted as a sport. As in Japan, drifting started out in the U.S. as an underground scene in the mid 1990s. Even today, there is a strong allegiance of serious American drifters who would rather you weren't reading this. But the popularity of drifting simply can't be contained.

You know you're popular when they make cartoon a out of you. Actually, **Initial D** *is a manga and anime series created by Shuichi Shigeno. It was licensed by TOKYOPOP (www.tokyopop.com) for an American/English language release. It focuses on Takumi Fujiwara, a Tofu delivery boy. Takumi (or "Tak" in the American release) has no clue he is the best drifter to slide through the turns of Mount Akina and that just about everyone around him happens to be immersed in the drifting subculture. There are DVDs, paperback books, die-cast cars, trading cards, a feature film, and video and arcade games dedicated to the drift phenom. The BitChar-G by TOMY is a little harder to find here, but you can pick up a similar version at Radio Shack (www.radioshack.com), they are called Zip Zaps. Here in the U.S., Jada Toys (www.jadatoys.com) sells various die-cast cars and model kits from the series.*

The early hardcore drift enthusiasts weren't waiting for the first D1, or Drift Showoff event to come to the U.S. They were taking their inspiration from the pictures of *Option* magazine, its spin-off title *Drift Tengoku*, as well as the ever-popular Option videos, and attempting to create their own version of the Rolling Zoku. American drivers began heading to the hills and deserted industrial areas of their hometowns to hone their skills as the pioneers of American drifting. All the while, this small group of rouge drift enthusiasts kept their newfound pastime under wraps so that drifting would NOT become too popular. They feared that ultimately it would become as commercialized as the tuner, or sport compact, scene. For these enthusiasts, the thought of a movie like *The Fast and the Furious* for drifting is sacrilege. Certainly they weren't thrilled about the first race in that movie's sequel, *2 Fast 2 Furious*, where the illegal street

drags were not only stacked four deep, but held on an impromptu road course through the city streets of Miami. In that scene, the cars jumped a bridge and "drifted" around any and every corner. *The Fast and the Furious* may have heightened the popularity of sport compact drag racing, but the sequel missed the boat when it came to drifting. Drifting doesn't need Hollywood special effects—it's exciting enough on its own. The third installment of the franchise called *The Fast and the Furious: Tokyo Drift*.

Drifting is fun, exciting, and you can do it anywhere with only a bunch of cones and a series of safety barricades—you don't need a multimillion dollar track to drift on, any large parking lot will do. The present popularity of imports and sport compacts makes drifting a perfect fit for the next major thing to grab the American public's attention and hold on to it for a significant amount of time.

Drifting Goes Legit in the U.S.

March 2, 2003, was the day when the drifting underground's worst fears came to reality. For all intents and purposes this date was when drifting really took off in America. If Keiichi Tsuchiya is the father of modern professional drifting, then Ken Miyoshi and his crew at Mainstream Productions must be drifting's distant American cousins. They hosted the event that put drifting on the map here in the States—The Falken Tires Drift Showoff. This was not the first drifting event on U.S. soil, but it was the largest to that point and it was one of the first that enticed some of the top drifters from Japan to attend. Kazuya Bai and Yoshinori Koguchi flew out and drove specially prepared cars, while Fumiaki Komatsu and Seigou Yamamoto were lucky enough to have Falken Tires actually ship their drift cars to the U.S. for the event!

Just as the Rolling Zoku did in Japan, early U.S. drifters honed their skills on winding mountain roads near their hometowns. Police, however, have no tolerance for illegal drifting here in the States. Driving like this in an uncontrolled

Continued

Drifter XL, a.k.a. Kasuya Bai, does what he does best on American soil—or blacktop, anyway. In the early days of drifting in the U.S., Japan's top drivers like Kasuya came originally for demos, and then to compete against American drifters. Here Drifter XL exits the main turn at Irwindale Speedway in his Tanabe S13.

This was a huge turning point for the sport, and not even Ken or Doug Stokes of Irwindale Speedway in Irwindale, California, where the event was held, could have known how popular the event would be. They figured no more than 2,000 attendees would show up, so if they got 1,500 people through the gates that day, the event would have been a huge success. Their calculations turned out to be slightly off, however. By 1:30 p.m. Doug had to close the gates as the number of attendees had more than tripled expectations—over 7,200 drift enthusiasts showed up! The event simply wasn't set up to handle any more people, so the promoters had to turn throngs of hardcore drift fans away. But this didn't stop those who showed up late from gathering outside the track fences to try and catch

The stands are typically packed at drifting events, but only Ken Miyoshi of Mainstream Productions and Doug Stokes of Irwindale Speedway could have known the first D1GP to be held on U.S. soil would draw a full house. They learned that the hard way when triple the number of spectators they expected arrived at the Drift Showoff they held a year earlier. With 10,000-plus spectators, the first-ever D1GP competition in the U.S. was the largest drifting event ever—including events in Japan.

environment is obviously dangerous, but with nowhere else to go, the first U.S. drifters took their inspiration from imported Japanese drift magazines and videos. Today there are far better alternatives like Drift Day, Formula D, and others—no one should ever drift on public roads like this. (Ryan Hill/Drifting Magazine)

a glimpse of the drifting action. It was an incredible event that helped pave the way for drifting in the United States.

Just as the automotive aftermarket in Japan took notice of drifting during its early days, so did various parts manufacturers in the U.S. The attention came mostly from businesses familiar with the tuner market, which was originally dubbed the import market, as it too hailed from Japan. Manufacturers that made sport-compact performance parts for every make from Honda to Ford tried to figure out how their products would fit in with the drifting audience. Various parts manufacturers even came out with drift-specific products and, if they didn't already have them, started making parts for the older, imported rear-wheel-drive cars that were already so popular with drifters.

Soon every niche magazine that covered sport compact cars saw drifting as "the next big thing" to happen to the tuner market, just as visionary publisher Daijiro Inada had in Japan. These magazines began covering drift events and running features on the 240SX and Corolla GTS. *Import Racer!* (now *Import Performance*), *Import Tuner, Sport Compact Car, Super Street*, and others tried to capture the intensity of drifting, which helped increase its popularity even further. Then a smaller company decided to take a huge leap by putting out a magazine devoted entirely to drifting—in July of 2003, Y-Visionary Publishing, which at the time put out *Import Racer!*, came out with the first-ever U.S. publication on the new sport simply titled, *Drifting*. I was actually co-editor of that magazine, along with Edward Loh, who headed up the special issue and is now editor of *Sport Compact Car*. After that, enthusiasts had to wait two long years before the title was put into regular production in December 2005.

On Sunday, August 31, 2003, things really started to heat up when the next big drifting event was held at Irwindale Speedway—but this time it was an actual leg of the D1 Grand Prix! This wasn't a demo; this was an actual points contest in the series. For this event, 16 of Japan's top drifters showed up to compete against each other and eight top U.S. drivers. For the historic first-ever D1GP held in the United States, no ordinary panel of judges would do, so a trio of

In Japan, Option *magazine has a spin-off title dubbed* Drift Tengoku, *which is dedicated to drifting. In the states, Y-Visionary Publishing, producers of* Import Racer! *(now* Import Performance*) magazine came out with* Drifting *magazine to do the same. This was the first-ever magazine dedicated solely to drifting in the U.S. At the time I was editor of* Import Racer! *magazine and co-editor of this special issue, which was headed up by Ed Loh— the same guy who judges Formula D events.*

It may have taken a couple of years, but Drifting Magazine *was finally put into regular rotation before 2005 was over. Editor Craig Taguchi has done an exceptional job of bringing the high-energy action sport of drifting to the static pages of a magazine by filling each issue with great photography, professional and amateur drift cars, as well as the appropriate tech articles, and more. Look for* Drifting Magazine *at your favorite newsstand and check out their site at www.driftingmag.com.*

Several of Japan's elite drifters showed up at Irwindale Speedway to do battle at the first-ever D1GP held in the U.S. Pictured from left to right are Kazuhiro "KFC" Tanaka, Nobuteri "NOB" Taniguchi , Nobushige Kumakubo, Youichi Imamura, Ken "Monkey Man" Nomura, and Katsuhiro Ueo.

Japan's elite drift drivers and competitive racers were called upon. Judges included Manabu Suzuki, Manabu Orido, and none other than the "Drift King," Keiichi "Dori Kin" Tsuchiya. This time Irwindale was prepped to accept a full house, and they got what they hoped for. Not only was this the largest event held at Irwindale Speedway to that point, but with upwards of 10,000 drift fans filling the facility to capacity (and possibly beyond, so don't tell the fire marshal), it was also the largest D1GP to that point—including events held in Japan! Today, we have a U.S. branch of the D1GP, which ensures

that we will not only continue to have these spectacular events, but also that they are held to the same stringent standards as the events in Japan.

Presently, the D1 Grand Prix is the premier drifting series in the world, but no more than a handful of events have ever been held in the U.S. during a single year. However, there are other organizations and event promoters who are putting on drifting events from one end of the United States to the other on regular basis. These include, but are not limited to, Drift Session (www.driftsession.com), DG Trials

(www.dgtrials.com), Drift Day (www.driftday.com), and, of course, Formula D (www.formulad.com).

Formula D

Slipstream Global Marketing, youth marketing agency and producer of car shows for the tuner market, launched the first official drifting series in North America dubbed Formula Drift, or Formula D, at the 2003 Specialty Equipment Market Association (SEMA) show. Jim Liaw and Ryan Sage are the visionaries behind the series. They started Formula D with a good understanding of drifting's popularity in Japan and its underground growth here in the States, a true passion for this new motorsport, and a bunch of credit cards. Putting the concept on paper wouldn't have been that difficult for anyone—basically,

Jarod "J-Rod" DeAnda is the voice of Formula D. He can regularly be found at drift events making himself hoarse from excitement. This photo is courtesy of J-Rod himself.

After winning the 2004 D1 Grand Prix, Yasuyuki Kazama took a sideways victory lap and did a series of smokey donuts. This was the first of two consecutive U.S. D1GP events he won.

The 2005 Formula D finals came down to a battle between two of the country's best drivers, Rhys Millen and Chris Forsberg. Their runs were almost too close to call when Forsberg's S15 caught on fire. The distracted judges were forced to call a "one more time," and both cars ran again—after the fire was extinguished, of course. During that run, the power steering failed on Millen's GTO, causing him to spin, giving the event win to Chris. However, Rhys was still the series points leader, giving him the 2005 Season Championship.

give U.S. drivers and enthusiasts an outlet for drifting much like the D1GP in Japan. Not only making this happen, but making it successful so quickly, was something very few people could have accomplished.

The duo didn't just pick up drifting after it came to the U.S.; Jim and Ryan were part of the scene even before starting Formula D. They brought some of Japan's top drivers and the Drift King himself to America for the D1 Driver's Search. This event was intended to find the best American drivers for the upcoming D1GP that would be held stateside in August. At that time, well before the Drift Showoff, no one on the business end of things really knew what drifting was, nor did they want to participate. Venues didn't want to take on the liability of letting people drive "out of control" on their property, and manufacturers didn't want to invest in something so physically and financially risky. Ironically, Jim and Ryan helped pave their own way and make it possible to hold drifting competition in the U.S.

These two guys were instrumental to bringing organized drifting to the States. R[y] Sage (left) and Jim Liaw (right) not only helped bring the first D1 event from Jap[an] the U.S., but they are the two people responsible for Formula D—the first official series in North America. (UrbanRacer.com)

It was Ryan and Jim's experience and the contacts they acquired through Slipstream Global that made all the pieces fall into place for both the early drifting events and, ultimately, for Formula D. To bring a sense of legitimacy to drifting they signed up the Sports Car Club of America (SCCA), which they had a long-standing relationship with, as a sanctioning body to coordinate the events and take care of event and participant insurance. This basically meant that anywhere an SCCA event

*Run 'em 'til they blow! Tires are expensive, and in drifting you will be using a lot of them. (Edward Loh/*Import Racer! *Magazine)*

could be held, a drifting event could potentially be held. On top of that, Formula D is held to similar safety rules as other SCCA events, and all Formula D drivers are SCCA members—their licenses are actually issued through the SCCA. Early on, Ryan and Jim also came up with some unique sponsorship including EA Games, which is the title sponsor of the Need for Speed Formula D series.

In March of 2003, a few months before the first drifting extravaganza at Irwindale, Slipstream Global in conjunction with Video-Option set up an open invitation event for American drifters, also to be held at Irwindale Speedway. This was more than just an opportunity for some track time, however. It would give up-and-coming drifters from the U.S. and beyond an opportunity to drift in front of, and possibly get noticed by, the hardcore Japanese drifters they had only seen on the Internet and in imported drift videos. This would not be an easy event to qualify for, as some of Japan's top professional drift series drivers stepped in as judges including, Manabu Suzuki, Manabu Orido, Dai Inada, and Keiichi Tsuchiya. When it was all over, only

eight out of 40 drivers qualified for the U.S. D1 circuit, including Calvin Wan, Ken Gushi, Bryan Norris, Hubert Young, Rich Rutherford, Ernie Fixmer, Sam Hubinette, and Dai Yoshihara. If all this sounds familiar to you, it should, because this all happened at the D1 Driver's Search—the same one I mentioned before. It would be a few months later that year when the eight lucky winners would compete against the top Japanese drivers at the aforementioned U.S. leg of the D1 Grand Prix.

All of this was the early groundwork that led up to the first Formula D event held in April of 2004 at Road Atlanta—one of four events put on that year. Events at Houston, Sonoma, and Irwindale followed on the schedule. In 2005, the Formula D series was expanded to six competition events including Chicago and New Jersey, as well as six demos held throughout the U.S. and Canada. This included stops in Denver, Cleveland, Milwaukee, Portland, Toronto, and a historic stint in Long Beach, where the demo was held on city streets during the infamous Long Beach Grand Prix. These events provided North America with an outlet for competition drifting

events and demos, where spectators could witness their favorite motorsport live at various locations. Formula D is also the focus of a G4TV show by the same name (www.g4tv.com). It was Josh Crane of G4TV who took notice of drifting and its growing popularity in the states and offered up a slot in the cable channel's lineup.

Formula D got even more exciting in 2006, as a seventh event was scheduled in Seattle and drifting on the streets of Long Beach was made an actual leg of the competition held the week before the Long Beach Grand Prix. Formula D also paired up with the Champ Car World Series to host drifting demos at Champ Car events, which introduced drifting to an even larger and more diverse audience.

In the beginning, Ryan and Jim created Formula D with a goal: to give top-level U.S. drivers a series of events across the country and an opportunity to grow their skills. They have done an exceptional job of that. Their future plans are to manage the growth of the monster they have created and make sure the series grows at the same pace as the drifters. This includes more TV coverage, more events, and more acceptance from mainstream motorsports. Along with their focus on growing here in the states, Ryan and Jim want to take Formula D global and have already licensed the series in Scandinavia and Australia.

Besides just thinking big, Ryan and Jim also have been thinking about the little guy, those new to drifting that want to be part of Formula D. This series really started at the top with professional-level drift events. But now it will be expanded to include small qualifying events where up-and-coming drifters will have an opportunity to qualify and get their SCCA Formula D license. This helps out newcomers by giving them a place to practice and safely increase their driving skills, and it also helps drifting competition grow in the U.S. by creating new drivers that will eventually compete in the pro-level Formula D events.

Drift Day

You can't go from driving your mom's car right into drifting competition. You have to start out slow, learn the basics elements of car control, and practice to increase your driving skills. Drifting is not something that anyone should be doing on public roads, but fortunately for everyone, there's the Drift Association LLC. Drift Association hosts Drift Day, an event where new and even experienced drivers can go to learn about drifting hands-on. The organization has been around and growing since 2001.

Drift Days are typically one-day events where different types of road courses are set up at given venues to offer track time to anyone who needs it. This includes everyone from beginners who just want to get a feel for drifting to competitors who need track time for practice and/or tuning before an event. Besides just offering a place to drift, Drift Day enlists the help of various experienced drivers to

Regardless of your skill level, if you're serious about drifting, you need to attend a Drift Day or similar event. There you can not only practice drifting on a closed course, you'll also get advice from top drifters about how to improve your driving.

offer drifting instruction and driving tips to anyone who attends. Professional drifters like Taka Aono, Alex Pfieffer, Ken Gushi, and many others will take the day to help people like you increase your drifting skills. If you want to learn how to drift, this is the place to start. On top of Drift Days, the Drift Association offers private lessons and even started a Drift Day Competition in 2003 that allows drivers to compete at an amateur level. All you need is a car that will pass a basic tech inspection, a certified helmet, and $100.

Drifting Competition Format

Unlike racing, drifting events have nothing to do with elapsed time or who is the first one across a finish line. Drifting is a highly subjective motorsport judged on show-

manship, execution, angle, style, speed, and even the amount of tire smoke generated. Drifting events take place on a winding road course that can be set up anywhere with only a series of cones to mark the track and some concrete barricades to keep the fun contained and protect the spectators. There are no power classes, and coupes drift right alongside four-door sedans. Although drift cars can be highly modified, in competition they must be based on production chassis and include an OEM dash. Having a few basic guidelines helps level the playing field and keeps the sport relatively affordable. Competition drift vehicles must also be equipped with basic safety equipment, and drivers must wear a certified helmet and a one-piece, fire-resistant, certified driving suit.

Tire smoke is one of the elements that drifting judges look for during competition—the more the better. The Hachi Roku and 240 put out their fair share, but nothing burns the rubber of a set of big rear tires like the torque of a supercharged V-8 engine. One of the first muscle cars to compete regularly, the Cooper Tires Trans Am is part of the Bubba Drift team. Knight Rider fans should appreciate the red bar between the headlights, but those of you don't know what I am talking about will have to rent the DVDs.

Once enough drifters are eliminated during competition in single runs, the best 16 are paired off to make tandem runs. This takes the level of difficulty way up, as the drivers have more to worry about than just clipping points, K-rails, and spinouts. There will be another car on the track whose driver is trying not only to out-drift them, but pass them as well.

Drivers use various techniques to initiate a drift at the beginning of a turn and various car-control techniques to maintain that drift through the remainder of the turn—the longer a drift with maximum angle is held, the more points are awarded. A driver can choose his or her own line through each turn, but points are awarded for drifting as close as possible to a designated clipping point located at the inside of each turn. Judges also award points based on style and skill exhibited.

Ultimately, in drifting competition, a driver's goal is to showcase his or her car-control skills. Drifting at speed, smoothly, with maximum slip angle, and coming close to the clipping point of each turn will earn the driver high scores. Failing to initiate a drift, making numerous corrections, and/or spinning out altogether will result in low scores. Each of the judges in the panel uses these guidelines at their own discretion to award points for each run based on a scale of 0 to 10. An average of these scores determines a driver's official score.

The competition format begins with drifters making individual runs to narrow the initial field down to the Best 16. From there, the group is paired off and two competitors are sent out on the track together to drift fender to fender. Each pair makes two runs so that both drivers have an opportunity to lead. All of the criteria from the single runs apply to these tandem runs, but ultimately the driver who is following wants to pass the leader to illustrate superior car control. However, he or she can only do this in the corners and while drifting. Passing under the right circumstances will almost guarantee a win. But because passing is extremely difficult, drivers will more often earn points on their following lap by mimicking what the lead driver does, and doing it as close to the lead car as possible. The lead driver can earn points by pulling away from the trailing driver—again, illustrating a superior level of car control. On the downside, pushing too hard and spinning out almost always results in a loss.

The judges use all of this information at their discretion to determine who will move on. When both drivers do an exceptional job and their runs are too close to determine a winner, judges will call for another run. The crowd usually chants: "ONE MORE TIME!" This can go on for several additional runs until one driver makes a significant mistake or their car fails. After the Best 16, winning drivers advance to the Best 8, then the Semi-Final, and Final round until only a single winner remains.

Drifting Into America's Future

Drifting's recent popularity spike here in the U.S. has contributed to numerous articles on the subject—not just in the niche automotive publications, but major news outlets like the *Wall Street Journal* and *USA Today*, as well as magazines like *AutoWeek* and *Automobile*. Even *Wired* magazine had to stand up and take notice, with an exceptional expose on drifting, titled "Go Skid Racer, Go" (October 2003 by Charles Graeber), complete with a side bar called "A Beginner's Guide to Drifting" by Edward Loh.

Without a doubt, drifting has grabbed our attention in the States—it has what it takes to be extremely big here. Not only does drifting have huge spectator appeal, it's also affordable to participate in, unlike many forms of racing. So what exactly is the future of drifting in the U.S.? Drifting will continue to grow at an exponential rate and American drift enthusiasts will add their own unique flavor to the sport. We will also see more domestic vehicles turned into drift cars. Of course, there will always be the drift purists who believe drifting is and can only be Japanese—this will make for good discussion in the drift-specific chat rooms, as will the drift-style cars that never actually drift.

We will see more American manufacturers produce drift-specific products, not only for 240s and Hachi Rokus, but for Mustangs, Camaros, and other readily available, driftable domestic vehicles as well. There will be drift trucks and possibly even some form of drifting competition for front wheel drive cars. Every publishing company will come out with their own drift-specific magazine and expanded TV coverage and merchandising are givens. Pro drifters will become household names as we watch corporate sponsorship deals and prize money steadily increase from event to event. We will certainly see more race-car drivers like Samuel Hubinette, Rhys Millen, and others take up drifting as it gathers momentum and mainstream appeal. Much of this is already happening, but there are no guarantees for the future of drifting. Ultimately it will be determined by our interest and enthusiasm for the sport.

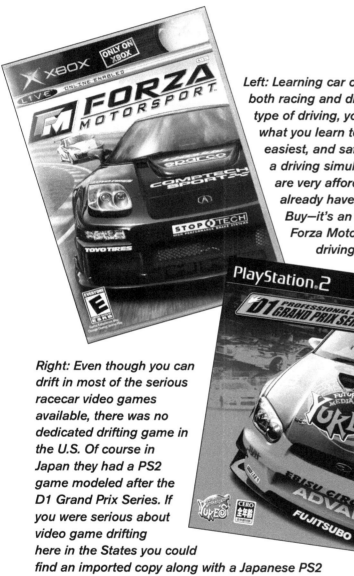

Left: Learning car control can benefit you for both racing and drifting. If you're new to this type of driving, you'll probably want to put what you learn to the test. The quickest, easiest, and safest way to do that is with a driving simulator. Believe it or not, they are very affordable and you might already have one. I got mine at Best Buy—it's an Xbox. I'm totally serious. Forza Motorsport is more like a driving simulator than a video game, and you can apply all the elements of car control when racing.

Right: Even though you can drift in most of the serious racecar video games available, there was no dedicated drifting game in the U.S. Of course in Japan they had a PS2 game modeled after the D1 Grand Prix Series. If you were serious about video game drifting here in the States you could find an imported copy along with a Japanese PS2 console to play it on (or "chip" a U.S. console so it could read the Japanese version). By the time you read this there will be a U.S. version of this game available for PS2.

Want to drift in your favorite professional car, on your favorite track, without a boatload of cash or any prior drifting experience? Then the D1 Grand Prix video game should be loaded into your PS2 as you read this. For those of you who don't recognize it, this is the first clipping point after the main sweeper at Irwindale Speedway—they even have the palm trees in the background!

In the D1 Grand Prix Series drifting game your screen will display vital information such as speed, engine RPM, boost (lower right hand corner), and even your slip angle (lower left-hand corner).

HIGH-PERFORMANCE DRIVING TECHNIQUE

Though a drift car may look like it's being pushed beyond its limit, it's actually being driven under very precise control. A car that has actually been pushed beyond its control limit will either spin out or slide in a direction other than the driver had intended, very possibly crashing into something. As you have no doubt seen in drifting videos and live competition, drift drivers can consistently slide smoothly and precisely through a series of turns, directing their cars exactly where they want them to go—how would that be possible without control?

maintain the lowest possible elapsed times. First and foremost, he or she must be smooth through the corners. Car controls are not on/off switches, and any racecar driver that treats them as such will not be driving as quickly as possible.

Because drifting is so exciting, and you see the car aggressively tossed from side to side, you may think smoothness doesn't matter. This couldn't be further from the truth. Just as a racecar driver uses his or her controls to affect elapsed time, the way you use your controls as a drifter will have a direct effect on your drifting. For a smooth, fluid drift, you must use smooth, fluid motions to control your car. All other factors being constant, smooth steering, throttle, and brake input will result in a smooth drift. Jerk the controls around and you'll be jerking the car around.

Not only will rough driving result in rough drifting, you won't have as much control over your car as if you were driving smoothly. You might think racing and drifting are two different things, that they're polar opposites, but this is not the case. Drifting is the same as racing except that drifters push their car beyond a race driver's ideal grip level to achieve the highest speeds and the lowest possible elapsed times. When you drift, especially at high speed, you must know and use the various driving techniques to maintain car control and you must implement them as smoothly as possible, just as a racecar driver would.

Let's break things down. Basically, you control your car with one rotating wheel, one lever, and three pedals. How you actuate these controls dictates the movement of your car. What you need to know about these controls is that the effect they have is relative to the input they

receive—so they are more like dimmer switches than on/off light switches. They are progressive. The pedals don't have to be all the way up or all the way to the floor to work. The more you push, pull or turn them, the more they will do. Conversely, push, pull, or turn them less, and they will do less.

Here is the important part: These controls will not only work better, but allow you more control of your car if you use every degree of their travel and do so in a smooth, progressive manner. Certainly this seems far too basic, but the fact of the matter is that people tend to think about their controls as either on or off: On the gas or off the gas, on the brake or off the brake, turning or going straight. When the average person (who probably doesn't know anything about racing or car control) thinks about going fast, they feel they must access their vehicle's controls quickly and aggressively—the faster they move, the faster the car will move. Want your car to go faster? Slam the accelerator to the floor! Want to make it stop faster? Stomp on the brakes! Want to drift? Just slam on the throttle, crank the wheel over fast, and yank up on the e-brake! See the trend?

Anyone serious about gripping or drifting has to know the proper way to manipulate their car's controls to get maximum control. This means providing the appropriate input, at the appropriate time, as quickly as necessary, while being as smooth as possible. This is something you can experience and practice in the car you drive every day on the street. Of course you have to obey each and every traffic rule, but that doesn't minimize what you can learn about using your car's controls.

Practice being smooth with your controls and balancing the car. Notice what effect each input has on the car—this works great in a stock car with soft suspension. As you step on the accelerator, the car's weight will shift to the back, making the rear end squat. Get on the brakes and the front end will dive. This will all be apparent even at or below the speed limit. When you corner, weight will shift to the outside of the vehicle and the car will lean in that direction. Once you experience all of these effects, work on manipulating your car's controls to minimize them. Not only will this teach you more about car control, it will make you a better, safer driver on the street. Besides, how you drive on the street

All of your controls affect balance and weight transfer when you use them. Stomping on the throttle will shift weight to the rear of the car causing it to squat. Notice how the fender is lifted farther off the front tire than the rear? This process will increase the rear tires' contact patch and thus, their traction.

Braking shifts weight forward onto the front tires, which increases their contact patch and available traction. At the same time, rear tire traction is decreased. This is the ideal time in a corner to initiate a drift because your ability to steer the car will be maximized and rear tire traction will be minimized, making them easier to break loose.

translates to how you drive on the track—both good and bad habits can be carried over from one to the other.

You have to not only know how to properly use your car's controls, but how much or how little to use them. As you drive your car, it will send you information that you can use to determine how much throttle, brake, and steering input you need to respond with. For example, how do you know when to shift? You listen to engine RPM and even feel it through the shift knob. You use this information, in conjunction with your need to accelerate or decelerate, to determine when you should up shift or downshift. Just as you have learned to use this information when shifting, you must learn to hear and feel the other valuable information that resonates through your car's controls and chassis.

Ideally, your drift car will have stiffened performance suspension, strut-tower bars and at least a race seat for the driver. Many drift cars are free of any extraneous interior parts, including the back seat, car-

peting, and even sound deadening. In a car like this, you can hear every rock that hits the undercarriage, you can hear your tires squeal as they begin to break loose, and you can hear any part that may have broken loose and is rattling outside the car. There is a wealth of information available if you just listen and learn to understand what each sound means.

Just as you listen for information your car is providing, you should also pay attention to what you can feel. Racing seats typically have minimal foam padding and are bolted to a solid frame directly onto the body or chassis. Vibration resonates right through all of that and into your body as you drive—sure it's not the most comfortable ride in the world, but it's not that bad either. You can learn a lot from what you feel because a drift car is more rigid, and there is minimal cushion between you and the road to soak up the bumps and vibrations. You can better sense the effects of weight transfer through the seat, feel your

front tires begin to lose traction through the steering wheel, and know when the brakes are getting hot by how the pedal feels. There is a lot of information to take in, so pay attention and do your best to figure out what your car is trying tell you. Once you become aware of the information your car is offering and learn how to decipher it, you can decide the appropriate input for superior car control.

Traction is the most important information you need to listen and feel for. There is no gauge to tell you when your tires begin to break loose, it's all about what you hear and feel. Racecar drivers must have exceptional traction-sensing skills so that they can use every last bit of available traction from each tire, at all times, without exceeding that traction to the point that they actually slow their car. However, sensing the available traction may actually be more important to a drifter. To initiate a drift, you want to dramatically reduce rear tire traction, and maintaining a drift depends on your ability to sense subtle changes in what little traction is left. Sensing and reacting to sustain this small amount of traction means the difference between maintaining a drift and spinning out. As you start out and practice drifting, pay attention to what your car is telling you. Listen for your tires to lose traction and feel how the car reacts when they do. Practice and experience will give you a good sense of what's going on.

Steering Input

Steering is a big part of drifting. Not only does the steering wheel allow you to point your car in the direction you want to go, in many cases it will be used alone, or on conjunction with other inputs, to initiate a drift. Ideally you want an after-market steering wheel that is round and has minimal bumps or contours molded into the hoop. Steering wheels with grip points or flat bottoms may be great for racing where the driver doesn't turn the wheel far enough to require moving his or her hands, but that's not the case in drifting. As an experienced drifter, you'll use every inch of your steering wheel hoop, turning it back and forth from lock to lock repeatedly. For this reason, you want a steering wheel hoop that offers good grip but offers a consistent thickness and shape all the way around.

You want to keep both hands on the wheel as much as possible, but you will have to move them around as you shift and turn the wheel to opposite lock. Of course, you want to provide steering input smoothly and progressively. You have to do it quickly enough to steer the car, but you don't want to do it so fast that you exceed front tire traction. As you drive at speed, your steering input can be enough to push front tire

traction too far—not necessarily enough to make the car lose control, but enough that the front tires can't do all the work you want them to. So your goal should be to provide smooth steering input quickly enough to make the car do what you need it to, but do it smoothly and progressively enough that your front tires can maintain traction.

Steering smoothly will benefit you in terms of balance as well. If you crank the wheel and turn in one direction, weight will be transferred to the outside tires. Do it abruptly and you can exceed traction limits of the tires that are receiving all that weight. Do it smoothly and you will progressively transition weight, and therefore traction, from one tire or pair of tires to the other(s).

Not only will you be turning the steering wheel from left to right, but you will have to bring it all the way back from opposite lock, or unwind it, which may mean turning it several full rotations. Thanks to their caster (the angle of steering pivot which geometrically positions the

tires contact patch behind lower ball joint), your front wheels will straighten themselves out when you are moving forward, if you let them. As this happens, allow the steering wheel to slip through your fingers and unwind itself as you slow down and exit a drift. Of course, you have to stop the steering wheel at just the right spot to aim the car in the direction you want to go.

Throttle Input

Yes, even though you will be breaking your tires loose, in many cases with the throttle, you can still use this control smoothly. I know that this may seem counterintuitive, but you have to realize that the throttle will do more than just spin the tires. You can steer your car with the throttle by increasing or decreasing slip angle with more or less throttle input, respectively. You can also balance your car with the throttle by easing off it to shift weight forward or easing onto it so you can shift weight to the rear. And, even when you do mash on the pedal, you can still do it smoothly. More importantly, however, is that when using the throttle to understeer, oversteer, Power Over, and increase or decrease slip angle, you must to do it smoothly and precisely. Roll onto the throttle rather than slamming it to the floor. Ease off of it rather than abruptly removing your foot from the pedal. Precise throttle input is the key to initiating, controlling, and maintaining a drift.

Brake Input

Slamming on your brake pedal not only goes against everything I've been talking about in regard to car control, but it can also get you in a whole lot of trouble. Although it

As this GTO is steered around a corner, weight is transferred to the outside two tires. You should use all the controls in your car as smoothly as possible to shift weight where you need it to make your car oversteer.

may seem like the easiest control to use (you just step on it to slow down, right?), the notion that there's only one way to use brakes can make them the most dangerous and difficult control to use in your car. Why? Because your brakes can do the exact opposite of what we want them to. What is your first instinct when you lose control of your car? Slam on the brakes, right? If you are going slowly enough, this might provide you with the desired result, but when you're traveling at speed, you have to apply what you know about car control.

Let's say you were attempting to initiate a drift at speed but failed and found yourself in an understeer condition heading for a wall. What do you do? Slam on the brakes to slow the car down, right? Well, no. Both braking and steering require tire traction and if you're in an understeer condition, that basically means you did not balance the car in a way that provided enough weight on the front tires for them to be effective (to have enough traction). Basically, the front wheels are turned, but the car is not headed in the direction they are pointed. Slamming on the brakes will transfer weight forward too abruptly, overloading the front tires, very possibly reducing their traction even further. On top of this, stomping on the brake pedal can lock up your brakes, making the situation even worse. Once this happens, you'll have little to no steering control, and instead of slowing the car enough to regain steering control, you will plow straight ahead in the direction the car was originally traveling—toward the wall.

If you do find yourself understeering towards the wall, you should gently and smoothly apply just enough brake input to shift some weight back onto the front tires. This should increase their traction enough

Racecars are set up with the ideal mechanical balance for their specific style of racing and exhibit minimal body roll. However, drivers still use car control techniques to balance the car and transfer weight for maximum traction. Here, the driver shifted weight onto the outside two tires for maximum traction during hard cornering. Notice that the inside front tire actually came up off the track. (Ford Motor Company)

that they can do their job and direct you away from the wall. More than just a pedal to slow the car, you can use your brakes to shift weight where you need it. But to maximize their effectiveness you have to apply them smoothly and precisely.

Left-Foot Braking

If you're going to practice this technique on the street, make sure you do it when there is no one behind you. The first time I tried left-foot braking I almost went through the windshield. Unless you grew up around kart racing, your left foot just hasn't been conditioned to gently press the brake pedal. Instead, your subconscious tells your foot to push it in hard, like you do to the other (clutch) pedal with your left foot. But don't worry; with some practice, you'll be able to smoothly brake using your left foot.

Left-foot braking is important for trail braking and to help balance

the car (trail braking is when you ease off the brake to minimize the effects of weight transfer after hard braking). Let's say you're in a corner and weight is shifted back enough to cause your car to understeer rather than oversteer. To fix this, get on the brake just slightly, but don't lift off the throttle. Of course, to do this, you'll need to use your left foot to gently apply just enough brake to shift weight onto the front two tires. Hit the brakes too hard and you'll further exceed front tire traction, making the situation even worse. If you're smooth enough, you can achieve the desired result and keep things under control.

E-Brake

Although this isn't something used by those who grip, the emergency brake, or side brake, is an invaluable tool for you as a drifter. The e-brake is a direct link to the rear tires and the rear tires only. Considering that breaking the rear tires loose is a big part of drifting, you don't want to be without an e-brake. I keep telling you to be smooth, and you do want to be smooth on and smooth off with your e-brake when using it to initiate a drift. But the goal when initiating a drift using the e-brake is to abruptly stop the tires from turning just long enough to break their traction. This means you want to pull up quickly and firmly on the e-brake and then release it— using it like and on/off switch. What can I say? There are exceptions to every rule. However, if you're using the e-brake to balance the car, the smoothness rule still applies. In that case, you would smoothly pull up on the handle enough to transfer weight as necessary, just as you would with the brake pedal. For drifting, you don't want the e-brake to lock into place every time you use it. For this reason, you may want to disable the ratcheting lock mechanism in your drift car.

Shifting

You know how this works; you just push in the clutch as you lift partially off the throttle and then move the shifter from one gear to the next. Of course, your shifting should be smooth. As you ease off throttle, you want to quickly and smoothly depress the clutch pedal. Meanwhile, take your right hand (assuming your car is left-hand drive) off the steering wheel and shift. Only take your hand off the steering wheel long enough to move the shifter quickly but smoothly. As you shift, lift off the clutch and get back on the throttle. This should all happen in one fluid motion. If you slam the clutch to the floor, slap the shifter into the next gear, and drop the clutch like

You will hear a lot about the ideal 50/50 weight distribution, which means a car is balanced perfectly front to rear. This may be great for racing, but in drifting, you want slightly more weight up front so that the car will have a natural tendency to oversteer. A set of scales like the ones at Technosquare in Torrance, California, make the job much easier, but you can tune your suspension at the track as well—it just takes some trial and error.

your buddy does in his street car, you can upset the car's balance.

Yes, even shifting can have an effect on your car's balance. When upshifting, it's easy to match engine RPM to your car's speed because you use one foot on the clutch and the other on the throttle. If you're downshifting and slowing the car with the brake, you'll come up one foot short for the controls. This is where heel-toe shifting comes into play.

Heel-Toe Shifting

To this point, I've told you that all the controls in your car can do other things than the one task they were designed for. For example, you can use the brakes to slow down, and the transmission can do that as well. Although it's true that shifting into a lower gear can slow you down, while drifting, you'll want to use the transmission to keep the car moving and only use the brakes to slow it down. Why? Balance, of course. Hard

downshifting can upset the car's balance just as if you were slamming on the brakes. Instead of using the transmission to brake, you want to keep both your flywheel (on the engine) and clutch plate (connected to the transmission) traveling at the same RPM.

To keep things balanced, racecar drivers came up with heel-toe shifting. Just as it sounds, you will use both the heel and toe of your right foot to control three pedals with just two feet. Apply the brake with the ball of your right foot. Then, as you depress the clutch with your left foot, pivot your right foot, while maintaining pressure on the brake pedal, so that your heel or the side of your foot is over the throttle. At this point you want to shift down a gear and, at just the right moment, blip the throttle to raise engine RPM—the whole time staying on the brake. At that point, you can ease off the clutch and maintain braking as necessary.

The small area of your tire that touches the road is known as its contact patch. The more of your tire that touches the road, or the larger its contact patch, the more traction it will have. The size of your contact patch is determined by tire size as well as pressure, vehicle weight, and weight transfer. This is a rough example of what a given tire's contact patch might look like under different circumstances. On the left, weight has been transferred off of the tire and the contact patch has been decreased, therefore it will not have as much traction as the example to its right. (Rob Benner)

The whole heel-toe shifting sequence should happen quickly and in one fluid motion. And, yes, you have to do it smoothly. Heel-toe shifting sounds awkward and difficult, and at first it will be. You need to work on this technique and get your timing down to the point that you don't even think about doing it—it just happens. Matching engine and transmission RPM will make your shifting smooth and help keep the car balanced. If you don't blip the throttle as you downshift, the slower rotating engine will abruptly slow the transmission and everything attached to it, including the rear tires, causing them to lose traction. Of course, in drifting that isn't always a bad thing.

Balance

Balance is extremely important for both racing and drifting. Very simply, a car's balance refers to the balance, or weight distribution, between all four wheels, front to back and left to right—also called corner balance. Of course in the real world, compromises with corner balance have to be made. Consider things like the battery, engine, fuel tank, and even driver and passenger placement. Automotive engineers do their best, but for perfect corner balance, you will have to take matters into your own hands. Before you get started, know that what may be ideal

corner balance for a racecar is not necessarily ideal for drifting. In drifting, you want slightly more weight up front to help give the car a natural tendency to oversteer.

One of the many reasons I chose a 240SX to be my personal drift car, and to be the project car for this book, is the fact that even stock it has very good corner balance. You can figure out the corner balance of your car, or the car you intend to build for drifting, with a little research or hopefully by weighing it yourself. Luckily for me, a friend of a friend had access to a set of scales, which is how I know my 240 is balanced within 5 lbs from left to right and around 185 lbs heavier in the front. That's really good corner balance for a production car, and it would not be that difficult to move some things around in the car to further improve on it. For example, mounting the battery in the hatch and swapping out the steel hood for a lighter carbon fiber piece would give it even better front-to-rear balance.

Perfect 50/50 weight distribution may be ideal on paper, or for a car intended to grip the road, but it isn't necessarily the ideal setup for a drift car. Cars with perfect or near-perfect corner balance, like the mid-engine MR2 or NSX, tend to understeer or push the front tires rather than oversteer or drift when driven hard. This doesn't mean those

cars can't be put into a drift, but they will have to be driven differently from a 240 or Hachi Roku because you will have to transfer weight forward onto the front tires with the appropriate throttle and braking response to compensate for their superior balance.

What I have been talking about to this point is mechanical balance—the actual physical weight distribution of your car when it is at rest. However, that is only half the battle. Your car may have perfect balance at rest, but the act of driving a car upsets its balance.

Think about the car you drive on the street. You know what happens when you get on the brakes: the weight of the car is transferred forward and the nose dives down. When you step on the accelerator, weight is transferred to the rear and the car squats. The same happens in left or right hand corners as weight is transferred to the outside of the turn and the car leans in that direction. Basically, every time you use your car's controls—steering, brakes, clutch, throttle—you shift the balance by transferring weight. This is a simple matter of physics and there is no way around it. However, you can minimize the effects of weight transfer and even use it to your advantage.

In road racing, the driver's goal to keep his or her car perfectly balanced. Since that's impossible, drivers have to settle for keeping things

Understeer is the opposite of oversteer, and although racecar drivers may use this technique, it isn't very popular in drifting. During understeer, the front tires don't have enough traction to turn the car around the corner and follow the ideal lines (see the darker lines on the track in the picture). Instead, the car continues on a straighter path, moving in the direction the car was traveling before the wheels were turned. Just as the rear end could come out more or less during oversteer, the front of the car may push more or less when understeering; it just depends on speed and traction. Racecar drivers have to be familiar with understeer as an element used to control their car. Drifters need to know about understeer in order to avoid it.

as balanced as possible. But why is balance so important? Balance translates to traction, and traction is crucial to going fast. Obviously, a racecar driver wants traction on the straightaways so he or she can transfer every last bit of power from the car's engine to the pavement. Balance is even more important in the corners, as it is the key to getting around them with the lowest possible elapsed times. The more balanced a car is in the corners, the better the weight distribution, and the closer each tire is to achieving 100 percent of its traction. Upsetting that balance can only reduce overall traction.

Of course, a car cannot be driven at 100 percent traction efficiency (100 percent traction from each tire, at all times), so a driver will have to make trade-offs on weight and thus traction distribution between the four tires. Ultimately, the trade-offs a driver makes will affect his or her

ability to drive the car to its full potential. Keeping that in mind, let's go over the Grip 101 example of what a racecar is supposed to do on a road course one more time.

A racecar driver will follow his or her ideal line on the approach to the turn-in point of a corner while on the brakes with the weight transferring forward. This means the front tires are loaded down, which will increase their contact patch. The extra weight on the front tires and their increased contact patch will give them more traction than the rear tires. At the turn-in point, the driver will smoothly come off the brakes and begin to turn the steering wheel into the turn (provide steering input), transferring weight, and therefore increasing the traction of the two tires on the outside of the turn, and at the same time decreasing the weight on the inside two tires. The driver will follow his or her

ideal line through to the apex, which is the point where he or she will begin to smoothly unwind the steering wheel and get back on the throttle. This ultimately results in weight being transferred back to the rear tires, which will maximize their traction and reduce traction at the front tires. This is the ideal situation for a straightaway where rear tire traction, and thus the engine's horsepower, can be put to good use.

Of course, this example takes place on paper in a perfect world. In the real world, it would be extremely difficult to maintain perfect traction all the time. So a driver has to maximize traction or use as much of the traction available from each tire. How much traction is available at each tire is determined by how a driver transfers weight as he or she drives.

But what happens when the available, usable traction is surpassed? Tires are not all or nothing;

There is no exhibition drifting in road racing. Racecar drivers will oversteer, but usually at a slip angle of between 6 and 10 degrees. Although this subtle slip angle may not be noticeable to someone who isn't watching for it, sometimes oversteer is crucial to driving through specific turns with the lowest possible elapsed time. A low slip angle allows a driver to maintain maximum momentum and engine RPM while turning around relatively tight corners at speed. (Mazda)

you can use 98, 65, or 23 percent of the traction you have available. The harder you push your tires, the closer you will come to their traction limit. Conversely, the easier you take it, the less traction you will use. As you reach the threshold of tire traction, you can exceed a given tire's ability to grip the track (to an extent) while still maintaining a certain level of traction and control.

Understeer

Understeer (the opposite of oversteer) is basically just what it sounds like—not steering enough. I don't mean that the driver didn't provide enough steering input, but rather that the car didn't turn as much as the steering input should have dictated. Let's say a driver was on the approach to a left-hand turn at speed and cranked the wheel hard to the left and then lost 100 percent of the traction at the front tires. With no traction, the tires would simply slide along the road surface

and the car would plow straight ahead in the direction it was traveling before the steering input was applied. This is an extreme example of understeer, as it would be unlikely to lose 100 percent of the front tire's traction.

Just as in racing, where drivers experience and even induce mild oversteer with a low slip angle, they will also experience mild understeer, and even use it to their advantage in the corners. This would be a very subtle understeer that would not necessarily be noticed by the average spectator. If a driver enters a corner and cranks the wheel over too abruptly and/or is on the throttle when turning, shifting weight off the front tires and onto the rear, he or she can exceed the front tire's ability to grip the track and thus turn the car. In this situation, where the front tires have lost a relatively small percentage of their traction, the car won't plow straight ahead, but it will not follow the tighter line that the dri-

ver had intended. Instead the car will push toward the outside of the turn following a wider path. To correct this, a driver needs to shift the car's weight forward onto the front tires to increase their contact patches and gain the maximum traction so they can grip the track and turn the car.

In racing, understeer is both an obstacle and a tool—it will happen in some cases when a driver didn't want it to, requiring a correction. It is also a driving technique that can help correct other problems—this is true for racers and drifters. While oversteer is exciting and fun to watch, understeer is not. If you are at a drift event and fail to initiate a drift, plowing straight ahead on the front tires, the audience will let you know how they feel about it. So why bring it up? Because if you fail to drift at speed it is very likely you will understeer. You still need to know what understeer is and know how to avoid it or recover from it—this is all part of car control.

Oversteer

If you're into drifting, you may already know that oversteer is when your front tires hold their path and the rear tires slide toward the outside of a turn. Initiating and maintaining an extreme oversteer condition, with a slip angle greater than 10 degrees, is your goal as a drifter.

There are various ways to induce an extreme oversteer condition, and they are listed in detail in the next chapter. Ultimately, they all rely on the partial loss of traction at the rear wheels. This is one of the reasons that many people think drifting is a loss of control—but this is not the case. When you drift, you do not lose 100 percent of the traction at your rear tires. You will reduce the traction to the point of sliding at an extreme slip angle, but you will retain just enough traction to maintain control of the drift. If you exceed that fine line, your car will spin out.

In racing, mild oversteer (between 6 and 10 degrees of slip angle) is used to control a car and help it turn around a corner. Once a driver turns into a corner, he may find himself in an unplanned oversteer condition if he comes off the throttle too quickly or gets on the throttle too much—either can cause slight loss of traction at the rear tires. Oversteer can also be caused by the driver turning too sharply or abruptly, assuming the front tires retain sufficient traction to do so. Oversteer may also be caused by heavy braking, which shifts weight onto the front tires (and thus off the rears). As mentioned above, shifting weight forward like this can correct an understeer condition, but it can also cause oversteer.

Oversteer can happen to a driver by accident (so he or she will have to correct for the condition), but it can also be induced purposely to achieve a specific goal. A driver can oversteer to turn the car around a tight corner where steering input alone would not be sufficient. A driver must also consider using oversteer as a trade-off between maintaining maximum tire traction and slowing down enough to clear a corner without oversteer, or just slightly sliding through that corner while maintaining as much engine RPM, momentum, and speed as possible. When used correctly, oversteer is an invaluable tool that can be used to score the lowest possible elapsed times. The difference between racing and drifting oversteer (besides slip angle) is speed. The examples above assume a racecar driver is driving at speed and right at the limit of whatever car he or she happens to be driving.

If you put understeer and oversteer together, you have neutralsteer. This is a driving condition where both the front and rear tires have lost some of their traction and are traveling at a given slip angle. This is also known as a four-wheel drift. Ideally, this means that the driver has done an almost perfect job of balancing his or her car and has pushed it hard enough to reduce traction at all four tires enough that they slide simultaneously, while still being able to maintain control.

Drifting competition takes the slip angle well past 10 degrees to showcase a driver's car control skills. Although drifting is not the quickest way through a turn, it's certainly the most exciting!

DRIFTING CONTROL

Although many consider it to be driving beyond the level of control, on the contrary, drifting requires absolute car control. In competition, drivers who advance to the top 16 are paired up and sent out on the track for tandem runs. One driver leads wh the other follows as closely as possible, attempting to mimic what the leader does and ultimately trying to pass. Driving in excess of 85 mph—sideways—is the ultimate exercise in car control.

The average person might look at drifting as being out of control. Even among those in the know, drifting is looked at in two distinctly different ways. There are those who feel it is driving a car beyond the limit of control, and there are people like myself who believe drifting is about absolute car control. This should be apparent from what I have written up to this point. You will certainly experience many different opinions on this subject. I am not trying to discount those people who are into drifting and don't share my beliefs. I actually think we are all talking about the same thing and are just explaining it in different ways. I attribute this to the fact that drifting is so new to the U.S. that there really has been no set terminology or consistent instruction to date. Hopefully this book will help start to change all that.

The best way to explain drifting is through car control. Remember that the first drifters in the hills of Japan were racecar drivers, and if you're going to drive fast on winding mountain roads, you had better know car control. Their original goal was to achieve the shortest possible elapsed time through various mountain passes. In search of their various cars' limitations, these drivers would push them harder and faster each run to the point that they began to lose rear-wheel traction in the corners. To maintain control, they would turn into the slide and drift the rest of the way through the turn. Originally, these drift pioneers may have thought this was the fastest way through a corner, but even after they realized it wasn't, they kept drifting for the sheer excitement.

Does this loss of traction mean their cars were out of control when drifting? No, the first drifters, and drifters today, push their cars past the ideal level of control for achieving the lowest possible elapsed time through the corners of a high-traction road course. But the car is not pushed beyond its absolute limit of control, as this would literally mean that a driver has lost control. When a car spins out, or a driver can no longer control its direction and smashes into the wall,

that driver has pushed that car beyond its limit of control. What this really means is that a driver has, in one way or another, exceeded the traction limitation of the tires.

Although breaking the rear wheels loose is crucial to initiating a drift, this does not mean there is absolutely no traction at the rear tires. Traction is dramatically reduced in a drift, but there has to be some level of traction or the driver would not be able to maintain the drift and would instead spin out.

Therefore, when drifting, rear tire traction is dramatically reduced, but not lost completely. When a car spins or slides out of control, rear tire traction has finally been reduced beyond the absolute limit of control. This is what makes drifting so exciting—cars are driven at the very edge of control; one false move will push the car over a very fine line and that control will be lost.

Skeptical? Try to remember and visualize the best drift you have ever seen—one car drifting perfectly, at speed, through a single corner. Picture it over and over in your head. Assume the driver is drifting as fast as possible, at the very edge of control. Now visualize the same car in the same corner, with all other variables being the

same—but imagine the entire corner is wet. What happened in your head? The car spun out, right? That's because the small amount of remaining traction was reduced by the water. If the rear tires lost absolutely all of their traction under regular (dry) conditions, but the driver was still able to maintain the drift, why would adding water cause the car to spin? It wouldn't, unless there was some traction left to be lost. Therefore, even in a full drift, at speed, the rear tires will maintain some small amount of traction—this traction is the fine line between drifting and spinning out. This is also an example of how drifting is driving at the very edge of control, and not driving out of control. Keep this in mind as you read what follows and try to remember the various elements of car control—both for grip and drift—that you have learned up to this point.

Initiating a Drift

If you go out to your first Drift Day and expect to just jump on the throttle, crank the wheel over, pull the e-brake, and slide through a corner, you will be very disappointed. Although doing all this can induce a slide, there's a lot more to drifting than just sliding your car sideways. There are a handful of techniques that you can use by themselves, or in conjunction with others, to initiate a drift. Car control is crucial to initiating a drift and, once in a drift, it becomes even more important.

Each of the following techniques is basically a way of reducing traction at the rear tires, which, along with the appropriate steering input, will induce oversteer. Some rely on acceleration to induce oversteer and thus are faster; others rely on deceleration and will slow the car while initiating the drift. For each technique, you will have to also provide steering input as you

Drifting may not be driving beyond control, but it certainly is driving at the edge of control. Even the best drivers in the world cross the fine line and spin out. This is a very rare sight indeed—Rhys Millen over-rotates during practice. He doesn't actually spin out, but slides sideways to a halt. He may have carried too much momentum into the turn, which brought the rear end around too far, or he may have applied just slightly too much throttle.

transition from the initiation phase to the actual drift itself, or the point where the car will take a set. Remember: you have to turn into the skid at opposite lock. If you are traveling fast enough to generate sufficient momentum to carry your car through the corner, and your front wheels are turning, the car will travel in the direction they are pointed.

One key thing to remember is that you want to look ahead all the way through the corner you are about to drift around. Be aware and try to take in as much visual information as possible, keeping your eyes on your desired exit point. This is important because you tend to subconsciously aim toward what you are looking at. That means you want to keep your eyes off the K-rail and anything else you don't want to run into.

In Chapter 2, I focused on gripping and finding the fastest way through a turn. This means driving at speed, or as fast as a given car can be driven under control. Not every one of the drift initiation techniques will require you to drive at speed. In

Drifting near the inside of a track, close to a designated clipping point like this cone, showcases a driver's talent. This is more risky than getting close to the outside of the track, however, because even a small mistake can cause the car to plow into the barrier, which isn't always made of hay bails.

Drifting is a display of driving skill and car control. Sliding at speed up next to the outside barrier of a track is a great way to demonstrate that fact. It's difficult to set the car up and drive it this close to the K-rail without hitting it, but at least the tires are constantly pushing it away from the wall.

Points are awarded to drivers who slide at maximum slip angle, as close as possible to a designated clipping point. It's extremely difficult to line up and drift close to one given point in a single turn. In competition, drivers must do this for a different clipping point in each of the turns on a given track. At Irwindale Speedway, this is the second of four clipping points that make up a single run.

You want to come as close as possible to a given clipping point to achieve the maximum possible score; you don't want to get so close that you hit it.

fact, depending on your car, you will typically run somewhere between 45 and 85 mph depending on how you plan to initiate your drift. If you are just starting out, you will certainly want to try the slower initiation techniques first. As you learn more and more about how your car reacts and feels while drifting through a corner, you'll be able to increase your speed and try more advanced drifting techniques.

The faster drifting techniques listed below may even require you to drive your car beyond its limit of control. Yes, I know this seems to contradict what you've just read, but let me explain. There is a fine line between drifting at speed (oversteering) and understeering—especially with a car that is not set up to drift and wants to grip or is prone to understeer. So in specific cases, with some of the more subtle initiation techniques, you will have to drive your car into a corner faster than you would be able to control your car through that corner. So I guess you are potentially driving your car beyond its limit of control. You will go just fast enough that the momentum generated when turning into the corner will cause the loss of traction and send the car into oversteer. The process of initiating the drift in this case will slow the car enough to bring you back to a level where you can maintain control throughout the remainder of the drift. This is extremely difficult because you can only go just slightly faster than your car could handle the corner. If you enter a corner much faster than that, where the speed scrubbed when drifting is not sufficient to slow the car enough so that you can regain sufficient traction to control it, you will spin out or crash.

Entry-Level Drift Initiation Techniques

E-brake—Slow Speed

It all starts with your e-brake—I don't care who might look down upon it. The e-brake is the easiest way to start drifting. This technique applies to drifting through a corner like this or just sliding around a single cone, so pay attention. The side brake, or e-brake, is your friend. By far the most common way to induce a slide is to use the emergency brake. Even if you weren't familiar with drifting before you picked up this book, you may have slid your car slightly sideways with the e-brake by accident—and maybe even on purpose (which explains why you bought this book)!

Using the e-brake to initiate a drift is common because it's easy to do and it's the one control that can send your car into a slide all by itself, as long as

you're going fast enough through a corner. Because using the e-brake to initiate a drift is so easy, and because it can be done at relatively low speeds, it is one of the best ways to learn. Of course, there are drift purists who look down on using the e-brake to initiate a drift. Because it is linked directly to the rear brakes, and the rear brakes only, the e-brake is a great way to break traction between the rear tires and the pavement. This makes e-braking seem like it would only be used by beginners—not to mention that it's a brake and does slow the car. Don't concern yourselves with people who look down on the e-brake—I don't! The fact of the matter is that all the pros have and use e-brakes, although they usually don't use them to initiate

a drift as much as to help adjust or maintain their slip angle. Rhys Millen even has a purpose-built hydraulic e-brake in his GTO.

You do not want to hold the e-brake up or, even worse, lock it in place. For this reason, the lock button can be disabled or you can use a Spin Turn Knob (you can find them on eBay for under $15) to retain the ratcheting lock function when you want it, and bypass it when you're drifting. However, you can e-brake anywhere throughout the turn. This does not mean you hold the e-brake throughout the entire turn when drifting a RWD car. If you start to straighten out anywhere along the turn, you can yank the e-brake to kick the rear end out, even if you initiated the drift with a different technique.

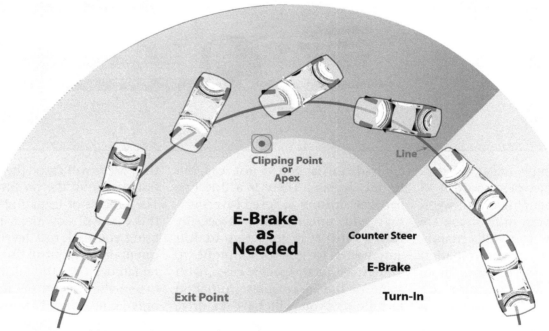

As you enter the turn at a moderate speed (start out slow and gradually increase your speed each time until you can generate and maintain a slide) turn in and quickly pull up on the e-brake just long enough to break your rear tires loose. The rear end will slide toward the outside of the turn. As it comes around you will countersteer—the front tires don't really change course but your rear end comes around. Notice that the front tires follow the line—your car will travel in the direction your front tires are pointed. Once the rear tires lose traction, you will want to provide sufficient throttle and steering input to keep the rear tires spinning and maintain your drift at the maximum slip angle possible. (Rob Benner)

Clutch Kick–Slow Speed

We have all "dropped the clutch" to spin the rear tires. The Clutch Kick method of initiating a drift is the same thing—except that you'll be driving through a turn when you do it. I know I said you shouldn't use your car's controls like on/off switches, but in this case you do want an abrupt change that upsets traction to the rear wheels. The great thing about the Clutch Kick is that you can use it at any point throughout your drift, even if you didn't use it to initiate the drift originally. The mid-drift clutch kick works the same way, sending a shock wave through the car's drivetrain that ultimately breaks the weakest link in the chain, which is hopefully the traction between your tires and the track.

Here's how it works: Push in the clutch pedal and disengage the clutch disc from the flywheel, which reduces the load on the engine. Stay on the throttle and engine RPM will rise quickly. Then let the clutch back out, dropping the clutch disc back onto the flywheel, which is now moving much faster. When the pressure plate forces the clutch disc back up against the flywheel, it has no choice but to slip or grab and transmit that energy back through the transmission, drive-line, and rear end to the tires. Ultimately, all this energy makes its way to the tires, which try to transmit it to the track, but the energy comes on so quickly that it breaks the tires loose—and that is exactly what you want!

Of course this is hard on your flywheel, clutch, transmission, driveshaft, rear end, half shafts, and tires. Drifting and racing in general are hard on equipment, so this should come as no surprise. This is one more reason to take good care of you car and its various parts with proper maintenance and upgrades where applicable.

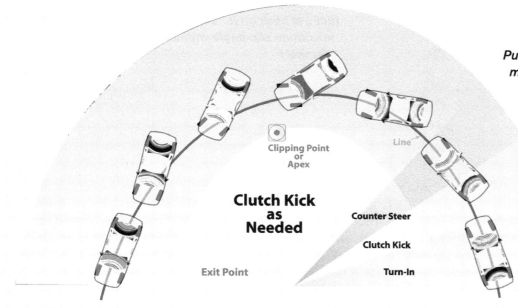

Clipping Point or Apex

Line

Clutch Kick as Needed

Counter Steer

Clutch Kick

Exit Point

Turn-In

Push in the clutch quickly while maintaining engine RPM (do not heel-toe), and then quickly release it to break the rear tires loose. If you're going fast enough, the rear end will come around and you'll need to countersteer and add throttle to compensate and maintain the drift. (Rob Benner)

Drift Drop–Alternative Technique

As we've discussed, initiating a drift basically is all about loosing traction at the rear wheels. Although you aren't likely to see many Drift Drops in competition, it is one way to break your rear wheels loose. To perform a Drift Drop, you can "drop" your rear tires (or at least one) off the edge of the track and into the dirt where they will lose traction with minimal steering and throttle input. The only real benefit to this technique is that it can be utilized by anyone with a low-power car and the resulting rooster tail of dirt can be a crowd pleaser.

Jump Drift–Alternative Technique

This is the same as Drift Drop, except that instead of dropping the rear wheels off the track into the dirt, they are dragged over the rumble strip typically found at the corners of racetracks. This causes the rear tires to "jump" and lose traction. Of course, this technique is only possible on road courses that have rumble strips.

Intermediate Drift Initiation Techniques

Power Over–Slow to Medium Speed

As the name implies, the Power Over technique is all about power. Basically it is a simple matter of the proper steering input and heavy throttle response. If your car has enough power, you can simply turn into a corner and hit the gas to break the rear tires loose. Once you do—you're drifting. Of course this takes horsepower and torque—lots of it. To use the technique effectively, you need to have more than enough power to break your rear wheels loose on command. The Power Over is very popular here in the U.S. where torque-heavy, often super-charged, V-8 muscle cars like Ken Gushi's Mustang and the Bubba Drift El Camino have plenty of what it takes to spin the rear tires whenever the drivers desire.

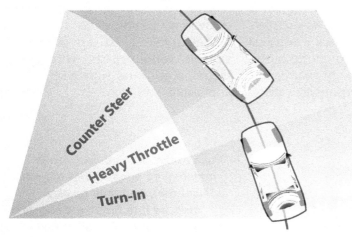

As you turn into the corner, stomp on the throttle to overcome rear tire traction. Once you've broken the rear wheels loose, you'll need to countersteer as the rear end comes around. Ease back off the throttle just slightly (but get back on if necessary) to maintain the drift at maximum slip angle without spinning out. (Rob Benner)

Shift Lock–Medium Speed

The Shift-Lock technique, like the Clutch Kick, uses the drivetrain to upset rear tire traction. Although it does require using the clutch, the Shift Lock relies more on the transmission to get the job done. As you enter a corner, you'll want to push in the clutch and downshift, in most cases from third to second gear, but this will depend on your speed, the corner, and your car. When performing the Clutch Kick, you let engine RPM rise and then drop a slower moving clutch disc onto a relatively fast-moving flywheel. With the Shift Lock, the opposite is true: you drop a faster-moving clutch plate into a slower-moving flywheel to achieve the exact opposite effect and get the same result—loss of traction. This abrupt change in speed is transmitted back through the drivetrain to the rear tires. The rear tires are slowed down quickly enough relative to the speed they are traveling across the asphalt and thus traction is quickly and dramatically reduced. Rather than making the rear tires spin faster, as with the Clutch Kick, you have slowed them down.

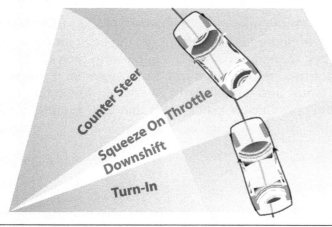

Turn into a corner at speed and downshift (do not heel-toe), causing the tires to slow down and ultimately break traction as you drag them. At that point the car will begin to slide and you want to squeeze on the throttle to get them spinning forward. The rear end will come around. Countersteer and adjust the throttle to compensate. (Rob Benner)

Manji–Straightaway Technique

Drifting courses are not always set up in the ideal location. In many cases, events are held on an actual road course with long straightaways—so what is a drifter to do? You can drive straight through and set up for the next turn, which is not very spectator friendly and will not earn you any points with the judges, or you can perform the Manji. Basically, the

Manji is a series of fishtails done down the straightaway. To perform this technique, employ a take-off off the Feint technique to slide the rear end from left to right with just enough angle to compress the springs on the side you are sliding toward. Then, as the springs rebound, you use this energy to bring the rear end back around to the other side and turn the steering

wheel in the opposite direction, starting the whole process over again. You will also have to work the throttle by easing on and off of it to pitch the rear end out and bring it back, respectively, in conjunction with the rebound of your suspension. You can keep this going for the length of the straightaway and only have to stop in time to set up for the upcoming corner.

Drifters who want to earn maximum style points on drifting courses with long straightaways can employ the Manji technique. This is basically a series of fishtails linked together down the length of a straightaway. Notice the trail of smoke and tire tracks left from previous runs where drivers made the most of this straight. (UrbanRacer.com)

Pro-Level Drift Initiation Techniques

Braking Drift–High Speed

As these initiation techniques require more and more speed, they become more and more difficult, which is just one more reason it is so important to know car control as a drifter. This move involves braking, balance, and relatively high speed. Unlike the previous techniques, the Braking Drift does not rely on a jolt or drastic change to upset rear wheel traction. Instead, it is an oversteer situation caused by unbalancing the car.

The Braking Drift technique makes for a very smooth and subtle transition into oversteer. If you're trying to achieve the lowest possible elapsed time through a corner, you would carefully balance the brake and throttle for a slip angle between 6 and 10 degrees. If you want to impress judges at a drifting competition, you will brake a little harder initially and then once the car has taken a set and you have made the transition from initiating to drifting, squeeze hard on the throttle for increased wheel spin to generate a slip angle greater than 10 degrees. Now do you understand why knowing the car-control basics of racing is so important?

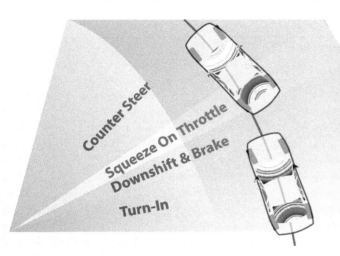

As you approach the turn-in point of a corner, you want to downshift while smoothly applying the brake. The best way to do this is with the heel-toe technique, which will allow you to be on the brake while maintaining engine RPM for a smooth transition shifting between gears. Braking shifts weight forward onto the front tires and off of the rear. At the same time, use the heel toe method to "blip" the throttle as you downshift. The weight transfer will put the car into oversteer and the heel toe downshifting will make for a smooth transition between gears. The smoother you can perform this task, the smoother your drift will feel to you and appear to spectators and judges. Then just use the throttle and countersteer to maintain the drift at maximum slip angle. (Rob Benner)

Kansei–Fast

Drifting with the Kansei style requires a high speed and of course, exceptional car-control skills. In fact, you'll need to be driving faster than you typically would with the braking drift or other initiation techniques—at a speed faster than your car could take the particular corner. The principle is the same as the Braking Drift: You use weight transfer to shift weight forward, improving front tire traction and decreasing rear tire traction. The effect of the Kansei is much more subtle, which is why you have to enter a turn with more speed than you did with the Braking Drift. Of course this also means, if done properly, the Kansei technique can make for a very smooth transition into a drift.

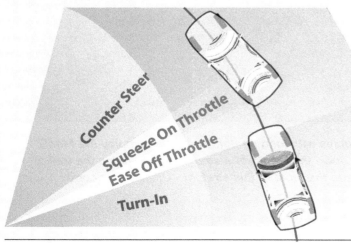

Start by entering a corner just slightly faster than you can actually drive through it. As you turn in, lift off the throttle to slow the rear tires and cause them to break traction just as in the Shift Lock, but more subtly. Once the tires have lost traction and the rear end comes around, squeeze back on the throttle and countersteer to get the tires spinning and maintain the drift. It's not easy, but it is smooth. (Rob Benner)

Feint–Medium to High Speed

Literally, Feint means "trick" or "maneuver," and it could be said you are tricking the car into a drifting maneuver in the opposite direction. This is one of the most aggressive and popular drift techniques used in competition and it's the easiest drift initiation technique to spot as a spectator. If you've ever seen a video or attended a live drift event where drivers enter a turn steering the car from left to right before they begin the drift, then you know what a Feint looks like.

Unlike the other techniques, the Feint was not adapted from road course racing, but has instead been adopted from rally racing. Rally drivers use this technique (aka: the Scandinavian Flick, or Toss Over) to help adjust vehicle attitude in the corners.

However, just because the Feint is a way to manhandle a car around a corner does not mean it can't be done smoothly. In fact, a driver must be careful not to turn the steering wheel too quickly or the car can lose traction at the front tires and understeer. How and when you begin your Feint depends on how fast you are going and the corner itself.

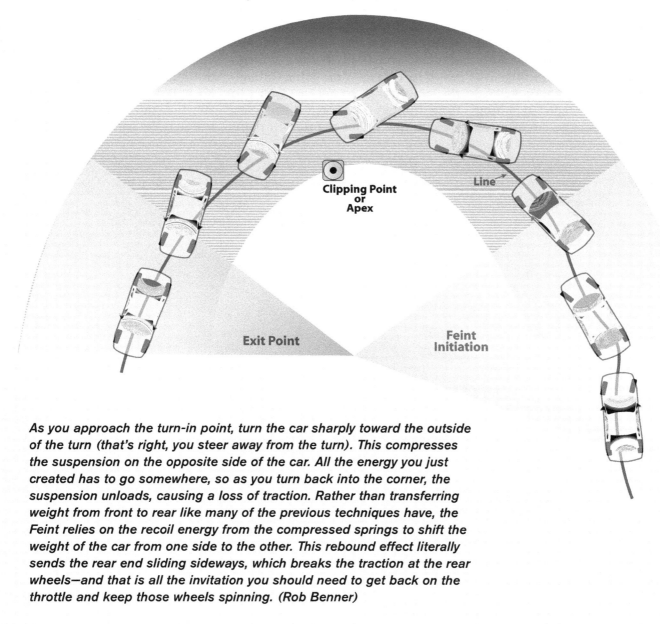

As you approach the turn-in point, turn the car sharply toward the outside of the turn (that's right, you steer away from the turn). This compresses the suspension on the opposite side of the car. All the energy you just created has to go somewhere, so as you turn back into the corner, the suspension unloads, causing a loss of traction. Rather than transferring weight from front to rear like many of the previous techniques have, the Feint relies on the recoil energy from the compressed springs to shift the weight of the car from one side to the other. This rebound effect literally sends the rear end sliding sideways, which breaks the traction at the rear wheels—and that is all the invitation you should need to get back on the throttle and keep those wheels spinning. (Rob Benner)

Other Techniques

Choku Dori–Extension Drift

Skilled drifters who want to maximize the time they spend sideways and impress the judges can choose to employ the Choku Dori technique. Literally meaning "straight-line drift," the Choku Dori is a way for drifters to start their drift early in the straightaway.

Remember how I said that using the e-brake was looked down upon as an entry-level skill? That doesn't apply when it is combined with other techniques for advance drifting like the Choku Dori. When approaching a corner at speed preceded by a long straight, pull up on the e-brake just long enough to break the rear tires loose and initiate a drift. At the same time, you need to provide the appropriate steering input to dial in maximum slip angle while keeping the car sliding sideways in a straight line down the straightaway, as opposed to sliding around a corner.

After you've induced a sideways slide on the straightaway and maintained it for the length of the straight, you need to carry enough speed to keep the drift going through the upcoming corner as well. To make things even more difficult, you have to line up for the turn-in point of the upcoming corner while already drifting at speed. This is definitely not your entry-level e-brake maneuver! Further complicating the Choku Dori is the transition between it and the drift that will carry you through the upcoming corner. If your car has sufficient power, and you are carrying enough momentum, you may simply be able to adjust your steering and throttle input, or you might employ one of the other higher-level drifting techniques like the Shift Lock, Power Over, or Kansei to initiate the drift that will carry you through the corner.

On the main sweeper at Irwindale, drivers initiate their drift early, performing a Choku Dori. This straight-line drift is done at speed to earn extra points and can be done on a straightaway or slightly arched stretch of track. Notice that the smoke trails behind each car are almost straight.

Switchback

Drifting around a single corner is fun, but if you want to drift an entire winding road course, then you need to master the Switchback. This is the technique that will allow you to seamlessly transition from a drift around a turn in one direction to a drift around another in the opposite direction. Remember that there's not a lot for you to do on a straight-away, and transitioning from a drift in one direction to a drift in the other is yet another way for you to show off your car-control skills. If you look through the first turn and set up your line correctly, you can initiate your drift at the right spot to carry you past the clipping point and through to the exit point, which should also be the ideal turn-in point of the next corner.

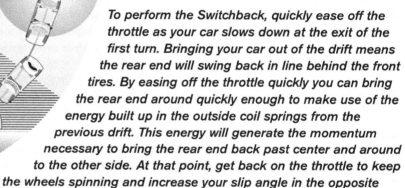

To perform the Switchback, quickly ease off the throttle as your car slows down at the exit of the first turn. Bringing your car out of the drift means the rear end will swing back in line behind the front tires. By easing off the throttle quickly you can bring the rear end around quickly enough to make use of the energy built up in the outside coil springs from the previous drift. This energy will generate the momentum necessary to bring the rear end back past center and around to the other side. At that point, get back on the throttle to keep the wheels spinning and increase your slip angle in the opposite direction. You won't necessarily even need to use an initiation technique if you were going fast enough to carry your momentum through the next turn. That doesn't mean you couldn't throw in a clutch kick, e-brake, power over or other initiation technique if you need to. Timing and throttle input is everything. (Rob Benner)

The Switchback isn't easy, but you can do it; it just takes practice. As you come out of the previous drift, ease off the throttle just enough to decrease your slip angle and yet still keep the rear tires spinning. After the rear end comes around past the center point, progressively squeeze back on the throttle to increase your slip angle in the opposite direction so you can drift through the second turn. If you get on the throttle too late, you may fail to initiate the second drift. Give it too much gas and you could spin out.

Maintaining a Drift

Maintaining a Drift sounds simple enough; once you've initiated a drift, all you have to do is turn into the slide and keep the rear wheels spinning. That may be true on paper, but there's more to it than that. As I've stated over and over, drifting is about car control, and you will never understand that statement more than when you find yourself traveling in excess of 70 mph, mid-drift, headed for the K-rail.

Just as there are several things that you need to do when you initiate a drift, there are several things that you need to do once you're in that drift. Your goal is maximum slip angle—the greater the angle, the better. But this doesn't mean your car is on autopilot. You still have to control the car by adjusting wheel spin to increase or decrease the car's slip angle and direct the car through the corner with a combination of the steering, throttle, and even brake input. You can control your car mid-drift with balance, or more accurately, by shifting balance slightly. The fact that you are driving the car through a corner with a slip angle in excess of 10 degrees already means the car is unbalanced—but that does not mean it's out of control. In this situation, subtle variations in balance will make your car do what you want it to.

Taking a Set

If all goes as planned after you initiate a drift, your rear end will be pitched out sideways and you will have turned the steering wheel to opposite lock—at this point you'll be drifting your car. It's possible to initiate a drift at just the right spot and at just the right speed to carry the car through a corner with little more than your foot on the throttle and

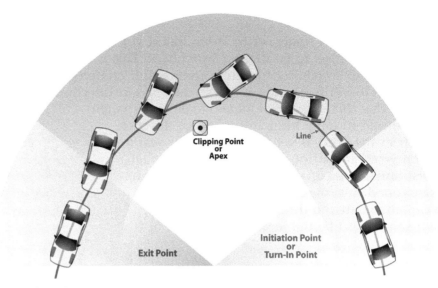

You can break down each turn of a drifting track into its turn-in, clipping, and exit points. The turn-in point is where you will use one or more of the initiation techniques listed in this chapter to break the rear wheels loose and initiate the drift. Just after that happens, as the rear end comes around, you will turn the steering wheel to opposite lock. At that point the car will have taken a set and you will be drifting. The more slip angle, the better. Smooth throttle, steering, and even braking response are key to maintaining a drift with maximum slip angle. Along the way, as long as your front wheels are spinning, your car will travel in the direction they are pointed. As you pass the clipping point you want to start easing off the throttle and unwind the steering wheel as you approach the exit of the turn. (Rob Benner)

You need sufficient power to break your rear wheels loose and initiate a drift, but it takes exceptional car-control skills to maintain that drift. Big-block V-8 power like that found in Ryan Hampton's Camaro makes breaking the tires loose very easy— and maintaining a drift very difficult. Maintaining a drift requires very subtle and controlled throttle response, especially with big horsepower, because you are literally driving at the edge of your tire's ability to maintain traction. If you apply just slightly too much throttle, or do it too abruptly, you will decrease the small amount of traction that is keeping your car from spinning out.

your steering held at opposite lock. But what do you think the odds are of doing that every single time you attempt to drift? Not likely—which is why you need to know how to control your car mid-drift.

In the initiation phase, you transitioned the car from a relatively balanced state (as you accelerated toward the turn-in point) to an unbalanced state, where you provided steering, braking, clutch, and/or throttle input to initiate the drift. Your car will take a set and settle back down after initiation of the drift, and once again be relatively balanced. Instead of accelerating toward a turn, however, your car will be sliding through it.

This may sound like a contradiction: "How can my car be balanced when it is in an extreme oversteer condition?" Mechanically, the car is unbalanced, as the weight is shifted forward onto the front tires. At the same time, some weight is transferred onto the outside two tires as the springs on that side of the car are compressed by the momentum generated in the initiation phase, which helps bring the rear end around. When you maintain this mechanically unbalanced state and minimize any additional weight transfer, you have taken a set.

Watch drifting either live or in videos and you can see the difference between the initiation of a drift and the car taking a set. You can see the weight being transferred forward and onto the outside of the turn, the rear wheels being locked up, and the front wheels being turned one way or the other.

When the initiation phase is over and the car has taken a set, all this stops and you can watch the car smooth out as it slides through a turn. In competition, the smoother the slide, the more points awarded. In tandem drifting, when both runs are so close who the judges need a

Rhys Millen's Pontiac GTO features these clear, sprint car–inspired lateral wings that run from his rear window back across the deck lid. They help keep the car from spinning out when Rhys pushes his GTO almost perpendicular to the direction he is driving, allowing him to achieve maximum slip angle.

tie-breaker, the driver who needs to make more corrections will lose the battle. Of course, just as in racing, where a driver has to make compromises in throttle verses braking for speed, as a drifter, you have to make steering corrections (using all the controls in the car) to maintain your drift and stay on your intended line.

Directing Your Drift Car

Your car will settle down once it has taken a set, but that doesn't mean your job is over. In fact, maintaining a drift is more difficult than initiating one. This is due to the fact that a driver must maintain a mechanically unbalanced state with minimal steering, braking, and throttle input. Even once you're in a drift, you still have to drive the car.

First, you must maintain the drift by keeping sufficient weight on the front tires and keeping the rear tires spinning at just the right speed. Subtle and smooth throttle, braking, and steering inputs are crucial to maintaining a smooth and fluid drift. Of course, at some point you need to adjust the car's direction so that you can drift all the way around

a given corner. You do this with the steering wheel, the brake, the throttle, and even the clutch.

Steering Input

It should go without saying that you can use the steering wheel to steer your car. Of course, you also have to keep it turned into the slide to maintain your drift at maximum slip angle. Therefore, you need to quickly, yet smoothly, straighten your steering wheel and then turn it back into the direction of the slide mid-drift. You don't actually turn as much as you make small corrections along the way. That means straightening the steering wheel out just slightly and then quickly bringing it back to opposite lock. You may correct two, three, or more times in a single turn. It all depends on numerous factors including your car, tires, speed, and the corner.

Throttle Input

This is where the interaction between your foot and the gas pedal is crucial. Remember: The throttle is not an on/off switch. Once your car has taken a set, the throttle may become the most important control in the car. Too little input and you can lose your drift. Too much and you can understeer or spin out. In between these two extremes is the fine line where you have the ability to control your car's slip angle and thus steer the car.

Ease onto the throttle just slightly to increase wheel spin, further decreasing rear tire traction, and you pitch the rear end out further, or increase slip angle. This also turns the car toward the inside of the turn. Gently ease off the throttle to decrease wheel spin and you will gain some rear tire traction, which will decrease your slip angle and straighten the car out somewhat.

In the middle of a drift, your wheels will be turned to opposite lock, so you have to steer with the throttle. Adding a little more throttle reduces tire traction slightly, allowing momentum to carry the rear end out further (increasing your slip angle). Easing off the throttle gives the tires slightly more traction and straightens out the car (decreasing your slip angle). This is not as easy as it sounds. It takes precision control to dial in just the right amount of throttle to achieve the desired result. It's very easy to come off the throttle too much and straighten out, or push down too hard and spin out. It takes practice to get it right.

Brake Input

Braking input is all about balance. Sure, using the brakes will slow the car, but just as with throttle input, there is a finite amount of brake input available to you mid-drift. Hit the brakes too hard and you can shift too much weight onto the front tires, exceeding their traction limit and pushing them into an understeer condition. You could also lock up the brakes, which can cause you to lose all traction and control. Do this and your car will slide straight ahead in the direction it was traveling when the tires lost their grip—which is a bad thing when you're driving through a turn. Use too little brake input and you won't slow down enough.

The bottom line is that you want to go easy on your brakes and use them to transfer weight when necessary, or slow rear wheel spin to help steer the car. Of course, the e-brake is very helpful in this situation as well. And although using the e-brake is frowned upon for initiating a drift, its use is widely accepted mid-drift to balance a car and control its direction, even among the pro-level drivers.

Clipping Point

The apex of a turn is more often called the clipping point in drifting. In racing, the apex is the spot at the center of the ideal line where the driver will come the closest to or "clip" the inside of the track. In drifting, the judges determine where the clipping points of each corner are and will designate them with a cone or some other marker.

Your goal as a drifter is to get as close to the designated clipping point of each turn as possible with maximum speed and with the most slip angle possible. To achieve this, you have to plan out your drift through a given turn from the approach. You'll want to enter the turn as close to the outside of the track as possible and ini-

Spinning out during competition means an almost certain loss—especially in tandem drifting where the goal is to keep up with the leader. It is, however, extremely difficult to follow another driver's line and do exactly what they do while drifting as close to them as possible. The added distraction of another car on the course is meant to test a driver's ability to control his or her car under pressure.

So, is drifting dangerous? Any high-speed motorsport comes with a certain level of risk, but overall, drifting is relatively safe. The cars aren't going as fast as they would be in a race and the process of drifting actually slows them down even further. Most drifting crashes involve a car sliding into the K-rail and then driving away. Taka Aono hit the K-rail during the 2005 Formula D finals and wasn't quite so lucky. He may have rolled his AE86, but thanks to the required safety equipment including a helmet, roll cage, and 5-point racing harness, he escaped this crash with nothing more than a bruised ego. Taka is a very aggressive driver and one of the best in the sport, but accidents happen.

tiate the drift at just the right point so that you can drift through the corner on a line that will put your car right up against the clipping point without actually clipping it—the closer the better, but don't run it over.

Exit

As you pass the clipping point you should still be drifting at maximum slip angle on your way to the turn's exit point. Drifting itself slows you down somewhat—remember that it is not the fastest way around the corner where there's traction. And if you're simply exiting a turn and ending your drift, you can ease off the throttle to further slow the car and gain more rear tire traction, which will decrease your slip angle and begin to straighten the car out. At the same time, you need to unwind the steering wheel to compensate for this decrease in slip angle.

How and Where to Start Drifting

So, that's pretty much all of it—but reading about it won't make you a drifter. Learning about the various techniques is a very necessary part of the process and it should give you a solid foundation of information on gripping, car control, and drifting to build upon. It should also make you think about how you drive and what you need to do differently to be the most dynamic and safest drifter you can be. Now you need to take what you've read and apply it in a real car, on a real track, which is the only thing that will actually make you a drifter.

Did I mention you should only drift, or attempt any performance driving, on a designated track? Drifting on the street is incredibly dangerous for not only you, but for anyone who happens to be around you. A huge parking lot without any curbs, parking blocks, or people is a great place to drift, but unless it's your personal private property, or you have permission to be there, it's not only dangerous but highly illegal—just like drifting on the street. Take it to a track or driving school; anywhere that you can practice safely and legally. When you first start out, "safe" means a big enough patch of asphalt where there is nothing close enough for you to run into, even though you'll start out at relatively slow speeds.

I will never forget the first time I really initiated a drift. I was driving in a circle in second gear at maybe 25 mph. I Clutch Kicked it and got on the throttle—the rear tires broke loose instantly. Just as soon as I did that, the rear end started to slide and it seemed like it was going so fast that it would never stop, so I frantically began to countersteer. I managed to ease off the throttle, straighten the wheel, and come out of the drift and exited the turn. I barely drifted for 1/4 of the turn. It was sloppy, rough, and I came back off the gas so fast that the tires grabbed the road really hard at the exit—but I did it. It felt incredible and I had a smile on my face for the rest of the day.

When you first go out to drift, don't worry about actually drifting. Just go out, be safe, and have fun. Try to remember everything you have read on gripping, drifting, and car control, but don't dwell on it—just keep it in the back of your mind. Start out slowly and work your way up to the point where you can actually initiate a drift and pull out of it. Keep doing that so you can a get a feel for how the car reacts to your input. How fast do you have to be going to make the car slide? How does it feel when it slides? How much throttle is enough to maintain a drift? How much is too much? Learn from your successes and your mistakes.

Once you have a car and a place to practice (remember: safe and legal), there are four basic things you want to learn—and practice over and over again. Start off with a 90-degree turn and then move on to a 180-degree turn, a 360, and eventually a figure eight. If you have never drifted before and have no idea of what a car should feel like in a slide, you can wet down the pavement just slightly so you can start out pretty much as slow as you want. This is also easier on your car and your tires. As soon as you are comfortable and gain some confidence, move on to dry pavement and stay out of the water as to avoid learning any bad habits that you will have to unlearn later.

When you start out, you may be nervous and fail to initiate a drift or spin out—I was scared when I first tried it and you will be too. Don't sweat it; everyone feels that way at first. All you have to do is make the effort and commit to pushing your car hard enough to break traction. If on the first few tries you don't go fast enough, keep trying and each time go a little faster until you do. If you do this and spin out, just dial back the throttle a little on the next attempt. Once you finally pull it off, you should be able to repeat what you did right. A lot of practice and some help from other drifters and instructors can help you drift at higher speeds and progress on to more difficult techniques.

You might even want to set up a video camera so you can review your practice sessions and see what your drifting looks like from outside the car. Just don't lose control and hit the camera. The only reason to learn and practice the 90-, 180-, and 360-degree turns is to get a feel for what your car will do when you drift. You need to know how much throttle, brake, and steering input to provide for the desired result, and how the car will feel when you drift. So, when you practice any of these techniques, pay attention and learn from each pass you make—even the mistakes.

90-Degree Turn

Set up a cone or marker on a flat patch of asphalt that is as free as possible of any dips or bumps, and make sure there is plenty of room around the area to spin out or slide. Accelerate toward the cone and when you get to it, turn into the corner, ease off the throttle, and pull the e-brake. As the rear end comes around, counter-steer only until your front wheels are pointed in the direction you want the car to go, let off the e-brake, and ease back onto the throttle. If all goes as planned, the rear end will fall into line as you drive out of the turn 90-degrees from the direction you drove in.

You can set up the turn in whichever direction you are more comfortable with, left or right, but as you progress, try the 90 degree slide in the opposite direction. This may sound simple, but to break the tires loose and make a 90 degree turn in the same spot each time may take you a few tries. You should also learn to clear a 90-degree turn using the Clutch Kick technique. This will teach you how your car feels and reacts when you initiate a drift, as well as how to make your car go where you want it to after you initiate the drift. The best part is that you can do it at slow speeds.

One of the easiest ways to get drifting is find an open area where you can set up a cone, or series of cones in a circle, and drive around it. As you go around try using the e-brake or a Clutch Kick to break the rear tires loose and get the back end to come out. Then countersteer and try to maintain the drift. At first, you will go in and out of the drift. It won't be pretty, but you can start to get a feel for how much or how little steering, throttle, and/or brake input it will take to drift. As your skills progress, you will be able to keep the rear end pitched out all the way around the cone for as long as you want, or until your tires give out. This is how I learned, and it's a lot of fun. (Rob Benner)

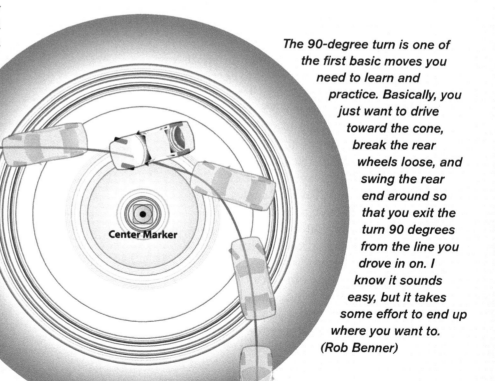

The 90-degree turn is one of the first basic moves you need to learn and practice. Basically, you just want to drive toward the cone, break the rear wheels loose, and swing the rear end around so that you exit the turn 90 degrees from the line you drove in on. I know it sounds easy, but it takes some effort to end up where you want to. (Rob Benner)

180-Degree Turn

After you have the 90 down, bring it around another 90 degrees for full 180. I'm not talking about drifting around a wide corner, but instead sliding your car tightly around a single cone. Just as with the 90, you want to accelerate toward the cone. Once you get there, turn in toward the cone and ease off the throttle as you pull firmly up on the e-brake. As soon as the tires lose traction, ease back onto the throttle just enough to bring the rear end around the cone and countersteer as necessary. This ups the bar as you have to provide just the right steering input, e-brake input, and throttle response—all at the perfect time. The payoff is that you'll learn even more about how your car feels and reacts when you drift—and this is a very fun maneuver to practice! Try this one with the Clutch Kick as well.

360-Degree Turn

You can practice this in two different ways. First: Simply expand the 180 explained above into a 360-degree turn. Use all the same techniques as in the 90- and 180-degree turns, but bring it all the way around so you exit the loop driving ahead on the same line you drove in on. The other way is to start near the cone and drive in circles around it. You want to gradually pick up speed as you attempt to initiate and hold a drift while going round and round the cone—you can actually start out with this technique, just like I did. Start out with the E-Brake and Clutch Kick techniques, and you can use the Power Over if your car has what it takes. When you get good at it, you'll be able to hold a drift around the cone as long as you want—or until your tires give out!

After you perfect the 90-degree turn, move up to the 180—it's more difficult and more fun. As you approach the cone, turn in and use one of the initiation techniques to break the rear tires loose. As the rear end comes around, countersteer to compensate. Your goal is to bring the rear end of the car all the way around so that you exit heading out the direction you came in. It's natural to favor drifting in one direction, so when you're practicing all of these different turns, make sure you put in the time to get comfortable drifting in the opposite direction as well. (Rob Benner)

Center Marker

The 360 will give you a good feel for throttle response and timing. Of course this is just an extension of the 180, but it will require you to maintain wheel spin and thus slip angle much longer. And, driving out on the same line you drove in on is more difficult than you think. As you master the 360, try hanging the rear end out more and more each time. (Rob Benner)

Center Marker

Figure 8

It was John Chambers of the Drift Academy in the U.K. that introduced me to the figure eight. Actually he called it a "Figure of 8," but I'm sure you get the idea. Basically you want to expand your makeshift 360-degree track into two equal 360-degree circle tracks—one right next to the other. You can designate a single cone for each circle; just place them far enough apart so you can drive a figure eight around them. Apply all that you have learned thus far and work your way into a drift around one of the cones. Then work up to the point where you can transition from a drift in one direction around the first cone to a drift in the other direction around the second, and then back again. This will teach you the finer aspects of the Switchback.

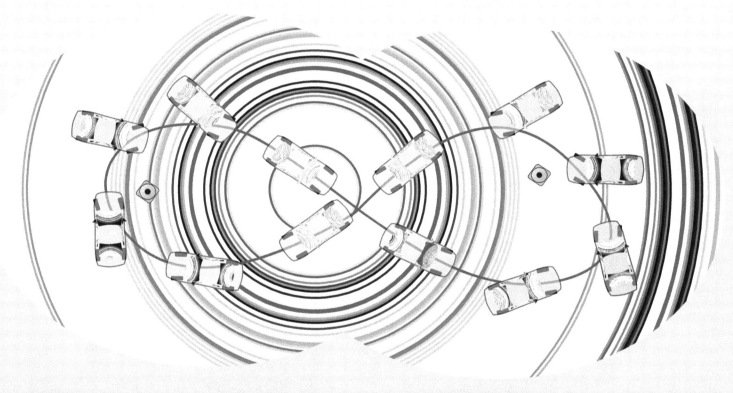

You've never had so much fun with two orange cones and a large open area of asphalt! The Figure 8 will help you get a feel for changing direction as you drift, which is better known as the Switchback. As you cross the center point take note of how the car reacts. The compressed suspension will recoil as you come out of a drift and help bring the rear end around to the other side so you can set up to drift around the second cone in the opposite direction. You want to start out slowly using the e-brake and/or Clutch Kick to initiate the drift in either direction. Then, as your skills progress on the Figure 8, gradually increase your speed and try some of the more advanced initiation techniques. (Rob Benner)

Beyond the Basics

Once you have the basics down, set up an actual turn made up of more than just a single cone. In the beginning, it's still a good idea to practice in a large asphalt area where there is nothing for you to run into, but eventually you'll have to drift through corners with solid barriers—so you better get your practice in while you can!

Using a series of cones, designate a basic U-shaped turn that is wide enough for you to slide your car through. Define both an inside and outside of the turn and make sure you have sufficient runoff room for an approach and exit so you can accelerate to the turn-in point and have room to slow down after you clear the exit. At this point, you want to practice drifting through the turn. Start out just fast enough so that you can initiate a drift with some of the slower techniques. Keep practicing this corner until you can regularly drift all the way through it in either direction. Then gradually increase your speed and try some of the more advanced techniques. As you get better, designate a clipping point and practice drifting as close to it as possible. Eventually, you should expand your corner to include a turn in the opposite direction so you can practice Switchbacks.

Ultimately, you should attend an organized event in your area like Drift Day where you can practice on a complete track and hopefully share your experiences with other drifters and instructors. Remember, only dedication, talent, and practice will make a true drifter out of you.

So how do I expect you to get all this practice in without a drift car? The chapters that follow include not only a breakdown of drifting's most popular cars, but a complete budget drift-car buildup with information you can apply to the drift car of your choice. Check them out, get your hands on a car, modify it appropriately, and get out there to put all you have learned to good use.

A seemingly unlikely candidate for drifting, legendary sport compact drag racer Stephan Papadakis has made the transition from driving in a straight line to sliding sideways in his AEM/Memphis Car Audio Honda S2000. Although there aren't many turns in drag racing (hopefully none) Steph was still able to draw from his extensive knowledge of car control, which has helped him set numerous records and achieve various titles in his drag racing career. These skills include, but are not limited to, accurate throttle, clutch, and steering input, excellent traction sensing ability, as well as an exceptional ability to read and properly respond to various input from the vehicle.

CHOOSING A DRIFT CAR

There are a variety of great drift cars available to enthusiasts here in the U.S. Since drifting is from Japan, it's easy to understand why the sport is biased toward imports. Today, imports still make up the majority of drift cars in competition, but domestic muscle cars like Rhys Millen's Pontiac GTO and others are making up ground. Their torque-heavy V-8 engines have what it takes to break the rear tires loose on command and keep them spinning.

I know there are some strong opinions out there about what's a good drift car and what isn't. There's also ongoing debate about weather or not front wheel drive cars can drift at all. With that I will make a seemingly bold statement: You can make anything with four wheels oversteer. But that doesn't mean any vehicle will make an ideal drift car.

FF Drifting

Can you drift a front-wheel-drive (FF) car? This is a question of much debate. It seems that there is no clear-cut answer because what appears to be a drift as performed by FF cars is not technically drifting. Basically, you can make an FF car oversteer by entering a turn faster than the car can handle and initiating oversteer with the e-brake, Feint, Braking, or Kansei drift initiation techniques. But because only the front wheels are driven, a Clutch Kick or Shift Lock won't work. Due to this fact, and because the rear wheels are not driven but dragged through a turn, it seems that FF cars can not perform true exhibition drifting. This debate will no doubt go

You can drift an AWD car, but it's not easy. It takes a lot of power to keep all four wheels spinning. For the first few major drifting competitions that were held here in the U.S., Rhys Millen competed with his AWD RMR Lancer Evolution rally car.

on for some time and, as drifting competition grows, we may even see a front-wheel-drive class, regardless of what it's called.

AWD Drifting

How about all-wheel-drive (AWD) cars, can you drift those? Yes, you can drift AWD car, but it's far more difficult than drifting an RWD vehicle. Rhys Millen, who is one of the best drifters in the U.S., and arguably the world, drifted his AWD

Mitsubishi Lancer Evolution Rally car at the Drift Showoff in 2003. Watching Rhys pitch that car sideways was impressive, and it was obvious that breaking all four wheels loose required a fair amount of horsepower as you could hear the engine sing when Rhys worked his magic. And because the front wheels are moving when drifting an AWD car, you can't corner at opposite lock as you would with a RWD car. You have to keep the front wheels straight once the drift is initiated so

Who says you can't drift an FF car? Certainly a FF car can be put into oversteer, but only a few of the drifting initiation techniques can be utilized to make this happen. The rear tires are not driven, but dragged through each corner. Regardless of whether you consider this drifting or just a power slide, watching an FF car corner with extreme oversteer is still impressive. (UrbanRacer.com)

steering, and ultimately drifting, is achieved with a quick snap of the steering wheel to adjust direction. After Rhys competed in the D1GP that year, the rules were changed and AWD cars are no longer eligible for competition.

Popular Drift Cars

For exhibition drifting, any RWD vehicle with sufficient power for its weight is an eligible candidate for a drift vehicle—it just depends on what you're comfortable with. By far the most popular drift car in both Japan and the U.S. is the Nissan 240SX. This is an inexpensive, lightweight, RWD, compact performance car with good corner balance, a 4-wheel independent suspension system, and a couple of more-than-sufficient powerplant options—the U.S. KA24DE and the straight-from-Japan SR20DET. There's also no problem finding aftermarket performance parts for these cars. Most drivers also agree that the 240 is an easy car to drift, which makes it an obvious choice for this sport.

Other cars commonly seen at drift events include the mid-1980s Toyota Corolla GTS (aka AE86 or Hachi Roku) or the Japanese Toyota Chaser. Mazda's RX-7 and RX-8 are a couple more contenders, as are the Nissan 350Z and the venerable Skyline.

Nissan's Skyline GTR makes for an exceptional drift car—if you can afford one. Other than price, the only problem is getting your hands on one. They were never sold in the U.S. so you have to import them from Japan.

But these aren't the only cars to be found sliding sideways around twisted road courses. American muscle cars like the Chevrolet Camaro and Ford Mustang can make great drift cars thanks to the fact that they are RWD and powered by torque-heavy V-8 engines. On top of being readily available, aftermarket performance parts for both of these cars are virtually limitless.

Believe it or not, trucks are another solid option for drifting. Although you don't see a lot of them at drift events, a compact truck with the right engine and suspension setup would be a great choice. Trucks are built on relatively rigid frames and have less weight over the rear wheels, which means the rear tires can be broken loose easily.

For example, an S13 240SX weighs just over 2,600 pounds and that weight is distributed roughly 53 percent to the front and 47 percent to the rear. On the other hand, a Nissan Hardbody truck from that era is just under 2,800 pounds, and the weight distribution is more like 56 percent up front and 44 percent in the rear. Having slightly more weight up front will make any vehicle more prone to oversteer, which could actually be a good thing for beginners who will start drifting at slower speeds. Plus, older compact trucks are not only affordable, but you could use one to get you, your tools, and a bunch of spare tires to and from the track. Still skeptical? Then consider that Nissan Hardbody

It was inevitable that someone would build a classic muscle car for drifting due to their tire-smoking power. But there's more to drifting than smoke. A car needs to be well balanced and have an exceptional, tunable suspension. This first-generation Camaro of Mike and Brendan Shannon was the first drift car built from a classic muscle car—and the first with a big-block V-8 engine. Because this had never been done before, they had to custom-build many of its components themselves. This takes, time, money, and extensive knowledge of suspension geometry. It also takes a very skilled driver, like Bondurant driving instructor Ryan Hampton, to handle a beast like this.

also comes with the same engine as the 240SX here in the U.S., the KA24DE, which makes it a candidate for an SR20DET swap.

Nissan 240SX (aka: Silvia, Sil-80, S-13, S-14, S-15...)

It has been said before, and I'm sure it will be said again: Nissan's 240SX is the most popular car in drifting today. Available from 1989 to 1998 in the U.S., the 240SX as we know it goes by many names and there are various performance options, both factory and aftermarket, available for them. What you get on your Silvia, and what you can get for it, all depends on what continent you're on—here's where things get a little confusing, so pay attention.

It all started with a name derived from Roman and Greek Mythology—Silvia. Originally, this was the name given to Nissan's luxury sport coupe of the mid 1960s. As there were only 554 ever made, it's safe to say you've never seen one. You can Google the Internet Nissan Silvia Home Page for more info on this now classic sports car, but this isn't the venerable drift car I am referring to. In 1968, production on the original Silvia CSP311 stopped and in 1974 the name was given to another Nissan, the Silvia S10, which was produced up until 1979. Then came

the S11 and S110, which were also known as the 200SX. Of course, you all know where this is going—in 1983, the S12 was born. Available in coupe and hatchback form, the S12 was known as the Gazelle in certain markets such as Australia, but in the U.S., the 200SX name was carried over from the S10 through the S11 and S110.

We finally got the S13 in 1988 (as the '89 model) and along with both coupe and hatchback versions, a convertible was added into the mix. Because in Japan the S13 was offered with the 1.8-liter CA18DE and CA18DET engines (NA and turbo, respectively), the S13 hatchback was known as the 180SX to the Japanese Domestic Market (JDM). Here in the States, we weren't lucky enough to get the turbocharged version, but we did get the bigger 2.4L KA24DE truck engine, which is why we know the S13 as a 240SX. At that time, the 200SX name was still used for various Silvias in other markets and carried over into the Sentra line during the mid 1990s here in the U.S.

Later, the 1.8L JDM power plant offered in the S13 was bumped up to 2.0 liters and the SR20DE and SR20DET were born. Although not offered in the U.S., the intercooled, turbocharged SR20DET engines are regularly shipped over from Japan

and transplanted into U.S. 240s, as well as other vehicles. Due to their vivid red valve covers, the first SR20DET engine that came in the JDM S13 is known as the "red top."

This leads us to the S14. Once again there were major styling changes, as both the coupe and convertible were dropped, along with the pop-up headlights. The S14 came with a longer wheelbase and the suspension was massaged for even better handling. The KA24DE in the U.S. and the SR20DET in Japan were retained with minor changes, including a toned-down valve cover that designates the later-model SR20DET engines as "black tops." The Silvia continued on through the S15 in Japan, but sadly its lineage ended for us here with the S14 in 1998.

Confused? That's understandable; I'm surprised even Nissan can keep track of all the engine and name swapping going on across the globe. But for us here in the States, there are really only two main Silvias that pertain to drifting, so I will focus on them.

Nissan S13 240SX

The S13 240SX was available from 1989 to 1994. You can call it a Silvia, 180SX, 200SX, 240SX, or even a Sil-Eighty, but these names all basically refer to what we know as a 240SX. Regardless of whether it's a

Hubert Young competes, and does very well, in this S13. Known as the 240SX to us in the U.S., our S13 features pop-up headlights that were incorporated to meet U.S. height requirements. Most are the hatchback models like this one, but a rarer coupe was also available. The S13 is popular because it has good suspension, is well balanced, and has numerous available aftermarket parts. It not only has sufficient power, but it's affordable as well. Notice how far the front wheels are turned. Even stock, the 240SX has a really wide steering angle, which is necessary to maintain a drift at maximum slip angle.

In Japan, the S13 Silvia featured fixed headlights and came in a coupe form—over there the hatchback with pop-up headlights was called a 180SX. Fortunately for U.S. and JDM enthusiasts and drifters alike, the Silvia front clip will bolt up to a 180SX (Japan) or 240SX (U.S.) with minimal effort. Drifters in Japan who damaged their 180SX front ends found it cheaper to install a Silvia front end, which is where the Sil-Eighty, or Sil-80, came from—part Silvia and part 180SX. Basically, a Sil-80 is the same car you see here, but with a hatchback. This combination proved so popular that Nissan actually offered it as a production vehicle in Japan for a short time.

The various models of the 240SX share at least some of their technology with the Nissan Skyline. In fact, they are so similar that the RB-series of engines found in various Skylines can be transplanted into an S13, S14, or S15. This includes the RB20DET, RB25DET, and RB26DETT (yes, twin turbos).

coupe, convertible, or hatchback, the only real difference between these vehicles is their headlights, taillights, and engine. The U.S. 240SX comes with a KA24DE naturally aspirated, 2.4L, dual overhead cam (DOHC) engine. Although they are regularly swapped out for the more popular JDM SR20DET or even the CA18DET, the KA24DE is a good choice for drifting. A single overhead cam version of this engine, the KA24E, was also offered in U.S. 240s. There are numerous aftermarket performance products for both the SR20DET and KA24DE engines and when properly set up, either will provide more than enough power to keep your tires spinning.

Basically, there are four different engines in a 240SX: the KA24E, with 140 hp and 152 ft/lbs of torque; the KA24DE, with 155 hp and 160 ft/lbs of torque; the SR20DET red top, with 205 hp and 204 ft/lbs of torque; or the SR20DET black top, with up to 250 hp. Obviously more power is always better, but any of these powerplants will work for drifting. It is very common to see KAs with turbo upgrades and even SR models that are massaged with various bolt-on performance parts and even upgraded turbos.

The S13's four-wheel independent suspension is also perfect for drifting and features McPherson struts at all four corners, which can be easily swapped out for fully adjustable coilovers. A factory LSD option can be found in various S13s, but if you acquire one without it, there are

Nissan's S14, like the one Conrad Grunewald drives, is also known in the U.S. as a 240SX. With this next generation of the Silvia, however, Nissan did away with the hatchback and convertible models, as well as the pop-up headlights. But, the KA24DE truck engine remained in U.S. models. Popular engine swaps for this car include both the red top and later black top SR20DET powerplants and even various RB-series engines from the Skyline.

plenty aftermarket LSDs to choose from. Weighing in at a mere 2,700 lbs, the S13 has great corner balance with just a little more weight up front to help the car oversteer on command.

The S13 240SX is so readily available and so reasonably priced, that I chose to build one as a drift car for this book. You can follow along in the later chapters and see just what it takes to turn an S13 into serious drift car.

Nissan S14 240

There's less to be confused about with the S14, which was available in the states between 1994 and 1998, but only as a coupe. Here in the U.S., the restyled S14 came with the 2.4L KA24DE engine, though the JDM SR20DET, in either red or black top, is regularly swapped into them. Even though the S14 appears bigger than the S13, it's actually just slightly shorter. However, the wheels were moved further out, stretching its

Chris Forsberg may have set his S15 on fire while battling Rhys Millen for first place at the 2005 Formula D finals, but that doesn't mean these cars are prone to spontaneous combustion. The S15 obviously came after the S14, but not here in the U.S., so if you want one you'll have to import it. The S13, S14, and S15 are all actually very similar. Engines and even entire front clips can be swapped from one chassis to the others.

wheelbase by two inches. With its "chunkier" styling, the S14 may also appear heavier than the S13, and it is, but not by much, weighing in at 2,800 lbs. The suspension remains a four-wheel independent setup, although Nissan engineers modified it slightly for better handling.

Nissan 350Z

Origins of Nissan's 350Z (aka: Fairlady) date back to 1969 when the '70 240Z was debuted at the Tokyo Motor Show. It was a huge hit. The Z line progressed to the 260, 280, and eventually the 300. Production abruptly ended in 1996. It seems you can't keep a legendary car down, though, because in 2003, an all-new 350Z was introduced, much to the

delight of Z enthusiasts across the globe. The latest of the Z clan is motivated by a VQ35DE 3.5L, DOHC, 24-valve V-6 engine, which puts out 300 hp and 260 ft/lbs of torque.

The 350Z's four-wheel independent suspension incorporates a 3-link system up front and 4-link in the rear—both constructed of aluminum-alloy components. This car even comes with a viscous limited-slip differential and Brembo brakes,

featuring 12.8-inch vented rotors and 4-piston calipers, if you buy the right trim package.

Professional drifters have said that even stock, the $35,000 350Z is

At 300 hp stock, the naturally aspirated VQ35DE 3.5L V-6 engine, which comes standard in the 350Z, is potent to say the least. Along with all that horsepower, it produces 260 ft/lbs of torque to help it keep up with the domestic V-8 muscle. Just think what this car would be capable of with one of the available turbo or supercharger systems. Notice that the 350Z even comes with a factory strut tower bar—and there's one in the rear as well. (Nissan)

If you want a new imported drift car with something larger than a 4-cylinder engine, you'll be looking for a Nissan 350Z. It's a really good choice for drifting because it has all the right parts, including rear-wheel drive, four-wheel independent suspension, four-wheel disc brakes, and a 300-hp V-6 engine. On the downside, adequately equipped performance models are quite expensive and are considered somewhat heavy at 3,400 lbs.

This car may look somewhat like a Z, and it should, but that's an Infiniti badge on the front. The chassis is the same as the Z, as are the performance specifications, making the G35 Coupe yet another eligible drift car. As of the writing of this book, it was rumored that in 2008 the new Nissan Skyline GT-R may make its debut on U.S. soil, although the Skyline badge may be absent. With any luck, the car will feature a twin-turbo VQ V-6 engine.

Along with performance engine upgrades, there are also numerous products on the market for the Z's suspension. You could get an aftermarket big brake kit, but why would you? The 350Z's Track and Grand Touring trim packages come with these Brembo 4-piston calipers over 12.8-inch vented rotors up front and 2-piston calipers over 12.7-inch vented rotors out back. All but the base model 350Z also come with a viscous LSD. (Nissan)

predictable and controllable in a drift. With stats like this, and plenty of available aftermarket equipment, it's no wonder the new Z is a fairly popular drift car.

Nissan 300ZX

If a new Z is a little out of your price range, you can take a trip back into the mid 1990s and consider a 300ZX. Many in the drifting community claim these cars are just too heavy at 3,300 lbs, but the same can be said about the 3,400 lbs 350Z. However, a twin-turbo '96 Nissan

300ZX coupe would be much more affordable. It's a pretty good bargain considering its 300-hp, turbocharged, 3.0L, 24-valve V-6 engine. Underneath it all is a four-wheel independent multi-link suspension system and viscous limited-slip differential, similar to the 350. For a car with this level of performance and plenty of available aftermarket parts, I would look past its somewhat bloated curb weight. You could always lighten it by gutting the interior and scraping up the sound deadening. The 300ZX was produced from 1996 back to 1990 and very few changes were made along

the way. If you look at one of the older ones and settle for the 222-hp, 298-ft/lb naturally aspirated V-6, the prices will only go down.

Toyota Corolla GTS (aka: Hachi Roku, AE86, Trueno, Levin)

You just have to love the Toyota Corolla—it's the little drift car that could. The Corolla is extremely popular for drifting, and with over 30 million sold worldwide, it's actually the most popular car ever produced. Of course, there are several different

How far back can you go in the Z-car lineage to find a capable drift car? All the way back to 1970 where it started with the 240Z. Although considered an impressive performance car for its time, the early Z engine can be swapped out for everything from an RB25DET Skyline engine to 7M-GTE from a Toyota Supra. Underneath the Z you will find rack-and-pinion steering, four-wheel independent suspension with MacPherson struts at all four corners, and disc brakes up front. An older car like this can take up a substantial amount of both time and money to set up properly for drifting, but it's possible. (UrbanRacer.com)

Available in a hatchback or coupe, the Toyota Corolla GTS is small, lightweight, and low-powered. That hasn't stopped it from being one of the most popular drift cars. The GTS has four-wheel independent suspension, four-wheel disc brakes, good balance, and those in the know say it's an easy car to drift. On top of all this, the "little drift car that could" has a seemingly limitless amount of aftermarket parts available for it, as well as several popular engine transplant options. And most importantly: it's affordable.

So why didn't the Toyota Supra make the list? First off, let me make it clear that this is not an all-encompassing list of the best cars for drifting. Instead I compiled information on the more popular vehicles used for the sport here in the U.S. to show what makes a good drift car. Even with more-than-sufficient power, four-wheel independent suspension, and four-wheel disc brakes, the Supra just isn't a very popular drift car. This is most likely for two reasons: 1) Price: Supras are very popular street cars, and that keeps the used prices up, and 2) Weight: the Supra is a heavy car at 3,500 lbs. But these reasons haven't kept a select few from drifting one of the four generations of Toyota Supras.

Corolla models that go as far back as 1966 in Japan and 1968 in the U.S., all the way up to brand new models you can drive off the lot today—the likes of which you are only going to see in the parking lot of a drift event. The Corolla I am referring to goes by many names, including its chassis code (AE86), its Japanese names (Levin and Trueno), as well as by its American title, the Toyota Corolla GTS.

Good things started happening when the fifth-generation Corolla was introduced midyear in 1984. This rear-wheel drive Corolla coupe and liftback were offered with a peppy 4A-GE, 1.6L, DOHC, 16-valve powerplant boasting 124 hp and a 5-speed transmission. Unfortunately, the honeymoon was short lived for the drifting community, as in 1988 Toyota switched the Corolla to front-wheel drive.

In Japan, Toyota's Chaser is a popular drift car, but of course we don't get them here in the U.S. You would think a seemingly heavy 4-door sedan wouldn't be the ideal drift car, but they have great suspension, good balance, and are available with a twin-turbo engine. And for those who don't feel that 210 hp is sufficient, the 3.0L twin-turbo 2JZ-GTE Supra engine bolts right in. The funny part is that at somewhere between 3,000 and 3,300 pounds the JZX90 and JZX100 Chasers actually weigh less than the Toyota Supra.

This car looks like a Lexus, but it has a Toyota badge on the front fascia. In Japan, it's known as the Toyota Soarer and can be found with either a naturally aspirated V-8 or turbocharged V-6 powerplant. What's great about this car is that you can buy it here in the U.S., as long as you go to your pre-owned Lexus dealer and ask for an SC400. The chassis is the same and we were even lucky enough to get them with either the 2JZ-GE 6-cylinder engine or 1UZ-FE V-8. Of course, this car will also accept an engine from various Soarer and Supra models, as all of these cars share similar engine bays and suspension. The IS300 (aka: Toyota Altezza in Japan) is another driftable rear-wheel-drive Lexus. With these or any luxury car, you have to keep both weight and price in mind.

The fact that you haven't been able to buy one of these new since the 1980s hasn't put a damper on its use by beginners and competitive drifters alike. The fact that the AE86 is cheap to buy, has a plethora of aftermarket parts available, and is touted as an easy car to drift makes it one of the top choices for a drift car. The drawback? They are getting hard to find and demand is driving prices up, but this shouldn't stop you from at least considering one for your first drift car. The GTS was Toyota's performance model, but you can also look for an SR5 Corolla. They look similar, but you'll have to put some work and money into the SR5 to bring it up to the GTS level. The ultimate resource for AE86 enthusiast is definitely www.club4ag.com.

Mazda RX-8

New, imported, rear-wheel-drive performance cars aren't that easy to come by these days. Mazda's RX-8 is

Although you don't see many in competition, the RX-8 has much of what it takes for drifting right off the lot. A few of its drawbacks include the hefty price tag, 3,000-lb curb weight, and perfect corner balance. Thanks to its lightweight RENESIS rotary engine, Mazda engineers were able to balance the RX-8 perfectly 50/50 front to rear. This is great for racing, but to make a car oversteer for drifting you want slightly more weight up front. Well-balanced cars aren't impossible to drift, but they require you to drive differently and shift weight onto the front end. And, although it revs to 9,000 rpm, the rotary engine is lacking in torque output. (Mazda)

There are pros and cons to just about every drift car. Mazda's RX-8 features a RENESIS rotary power plant that produces 238 hp and is capable of spinning at 9,000 rpm, its chassis is perfectly balanced and sits atop exceptional suspension. The downside for the latest in the RX lineup is the fact that rotary engines aren't known for their torque, and the car has a price tag starting in the $30s. However, these two factors haven't kept the RX-8 from drifting competitively. (UrbanRacer.com)

bone up front and multi-link out back, and all trim packages come standard with a Tochigi-Fuji torque-sensing limited-slip differential. If all this has you ready to pick one up, the top-of-the-line RX-8, 6-speed Shinka model sells brand new for just over $33K.

Mazda RX-7

Before the RX-8, there was Mazda's ultra-sexy, third-generation RX-7 (chassis code FD3S), which was available in the U.S. from 1993 to 1995. The third-gen RX-7 comes standard with four-wheel-independent McPherson strut suspension, four-wheel disc brakes, a 5-speed manual transmission, and a limited-slip differential. However, the most impressive aspect of the last-generation RX-7 was its 13B-REW twin-sequential-turbocharged rotary engine, which pro-

one of the few on the market. The next generation of the RX line gets its zoom (both of them, actually) from a 1.3L, RENESIS, 2-rotor rotary engine coupled to a 6-speed manual transmission. With this new engine series, Mazda wanted to improve on its infamous 13B-REW turbocharged rotary while actually reducing emissions—a difficult task to say the least. Of course, the Mazda engineers are pretty crafty and managed get 238 hp and 159 ft/lbs of torque out of the six-intake-port RENESIS. Even more impressive is the fact that this engine redlines all the way up at 9,000 rpm—and the designers made all this happen without a turbo! This lightweight engine also helped Mazda engineers to balance the just-over-3,000-lb car perfectly front to rear, just as they had with the previous-generation RX-7. Along with all this, the car rides on 4-wheel independent suspension, double wish-

Relatively low torque or not, the third-generation RX-7 can still hang with the rod-and-piston set. With the addition of fully adjustable coilovers and maybe a little weight shifting, drifters can make the RX-7 and RX-8 easier to oversteer. With similar specs, a twin-turbo '95 RX-7 goes for much less than a new RX-8, which may explain its popularity. The fact that it's turbocharged probably doesn't hurt either.

Are you asking yourself, "What the heck is a rotary, anyway?" Well, this is it. That rounded triangle in the middle is the rotor. It "wobbles" around in the elongated round housing while turning an eccentric shaft at the center. At each of the three corners there is an apex seal and all three are always in contact with the housing. Each of the three sides is like the top of a piston, but instead of moving through four strokes, combustion will push one edge right after the other in quick repetition, which is why the rotary is capable of such high RPM. (Mazda)

If price is the only thing keeping you out of an RX-series Mazda, then you need to consider one of the older RX-7s. You can pick up a second-generation RX-7 with a turbocharged 13B at an S13 price. One drawback is that there aren't as many aftermarket performance parts available for them, but you should be able to find what you need.

duced 255 hp and sustained a staggering 8,000-rpm redline! Mazda is known for its rotary-engine expertise and is the first and only manufacturer to put this unique powerplant into production automobiles, starting with the Cosmo Sport in 1967.

The third-gen RX-7 may not be much for interior accommodations, but what it lacks in comfort it more than makes up for in performance—which is exactly what it was designed to do. Along with the impressive engine output, the other benefit of the rotary is its light weight. Because of its small size and the fact that it's made up of fewer parts than a traditional piston engine of similar power, the RX-7's rotary is much lighter, which

For drifters on a really tight budget, Mazda's first-generation RX-7 is an affordable option as long as you do your homework before you buy. Many come with drum brakes, an open differential, and a 12A engine. However, 1984 or newer GSL-SE models feature a 13B engine, 30 extra hp, four-wheel disc brakes, and even an LSD. (UrbanRacer.com)

allowed engineers to balance the car exceptionally well. Of course, there is also a drawback to rotary power—

a serious lack of torque. It seems the cost for that high-revving, 8,000-rpm redline was the tire-smoking torque required to break tires loose, especially in the lower RPM range. This means to drift the RX-7, a driver will have to keep the RPM, and thus speed, up, which is not necessarily ideal for the beginner.

Rotary engines also have a reputation for being temperamental, which could be because they're so unique. When you're out driving, you can be pretty sure the car next to you has a traditional piston engine, unless it just happens to be an RX-7, an RX-8, or you happen to spot a Cosmo. The fact that the rotary powerplant is so unique means it has its own unique set of quirks. And if you want to drift an RX-7, you'll need to learn them so you can know what to expect. There are those who claim that you'll have to throw a bunch of money at a rotary engine just to keep it running right under harsh conditions like racing or drifting. Of course, others say that this is no more the case with a rotary engine than it is with a traditional piston engine.

Third-gen RX-7s are somewhat rare and relatively expensive for their age, but there are other options where RX-7s are concerned. The second-generation RX-7, although not as stylish, can be found for a very reasonable sum and come equipped with all the performance options you could ask for on a production car. From 1986 to 1988, a 146-hp 13B rotary engine came standard and a factory turbocharged 182-hp option known as the Turbo II was available. From 1989 through 1991, the naturally aspirated engine's horsepower was upped to 160 hp, while the turbo jumped to 200 hp! All of the second-gen RX-7s came standard with a 5-speed transmission and 4-wheel-disc brakes. Certain trim levels even included four-piston front brake calipers and

a limited-slip differential. These cars also boast a four-wheel independent McPherson strut suspension.

Although the first-generation RX-7 was heralded by the automotive media as a groundbreaking sports car, it isn't the ideal drifter. Early base models featured a 12A rotary engine with only 1.2 liters of displacement and 105 hp. Other drawbacks are that only the most high-end models came with four-wheel disc brakes, and the rear suspension is made up of a live axle with coil springs, as opposed to the independent rear suspension of later models. It also came with a recirculating-ball steering system that even automotive journalists who loved the car didn't like. Yet another drawback is that there aren't that many aftermarket performance parts for this early RX-7. This is not to say you can't drift the first-gen RX-7, just that it might

not be your best choice. But if you're set on this car, look for an '84 or newer GSL-SE model as it will have the first of the 13B engines, which came with 135 hp as well as four-wheel disc brakes and a limited-slip differential.

Mazda Miata

It may seem like an unlikely candidate, but the Mazda Miata is a solid choice for drifting and it's not uncommon to see them at drift events. You may look at the Miata and see a college girl's car, but the same thing can be said about the Corolla, and that hasn't made anyone in drifting shy away from it. Like the Corolla, Miatas are moderately powered and have a short wheelbase, which seem to be drawbacks, but again, these stats haven't hurt the Corolla.

What's great about the Miata is that it was designed as a performance

By this point you should be aware that for drifting you want a car with a good suspension that is well balanced, has a good power-to-weight ratio, and has a variety of available aftermarket performance parts. You can apply all of this to the Mazda Miata—plus you can pick a new one up for under $25K. Because it's a convertible, it really makes sense to put a roll cage and 5-point harnesses in your Miata if you plan to go drifting. (Mazda)

Just like the Nissan 240SX and Toyota Corolla, the lightweight and affordable Mazda Miata makes a great car for the beginner. There's enough power to break the rear tires loose, but even at full throttle there isn't so much power that you'll get yourself in serious trouble—of course you still want to practice drifting with extreme caution. As your skills progress, you can increase the power with a turbo kit or supercharger, and there are plenty of suspension components available so that you can set up the little Mazda to handle however you like. (Antony Fraser)

roadster. Although you can get a fully loaded Miata with power locks, power windows, and an automatic transmission, base models come without such equipment. The Miata's lightweight unibody comes complete with Mazda's Power Plant Frame (PPF), which reinforces what could be an otherwise flexible chassis by adding a more traditional frame section between the engine and rear axle. On top of that (or, more accurately, underneath) Mazda engineers designed a four-wheel independent suspension for the Miata and distributed weight carefully throughout the car to achieve near perfect balance front to rear. When you consider all this, the fact that you can get a Miata with a limited-slip differential and no traction control, it's clear that its engineers designed it with an appreciation for the power slide.

The infamous Toyota Corolla GTS may share a few of the limita-

tions and some of the benefits of the Mazda Miata, but the Miata possesses one distinct advantage. The Corolla GTS was only produced between 1984 and 1987, so there are a limited number of them available. The first-generation Mazda Miata MX-5 was introduced in 1989 as a '90 model, and although it has gone through various revisions through the years, this performance-minded roadster has remained pretty much the same through 2005.

If you are considering a Miata as a drift car, here are few things to look for. The 1990 to '98 Miata is known as the NA. From 1990 to 1993, the MX-5 came with the 120-hp 1.6L engine. These are the least desirable years for the Miata due to the smaller engine and the lack of a limited-slip option—although no one says you can't modify one to suit your needs. In 1994, things started to look up, as a 133-hp 1.8L BP engine and a fac-

tory limited-slip differential became available. NA trim packages to look for are A, B, and R packages, while the C Package and M Edition aren't necessarily what you want for drifting. A was the base model, while B offered moderate options. R stands for the aptly named Race Package. The C Package and the M Edition come with a host of creature comfort options you don't necessarily need, including slippery leather seats, and they're also the most likely to have automatic transmissions.

In 1999, the Mazda released a revised Miata known as the NB, also known as the Mark II. The body changed for the better and the little Miata began to look a lot more like its big brother, the RX-7. But the NB was more than just a facelift. The BP engine was tweaked slightly and dubbed the BP-4W, which is known for its increased cylinder-head flow and makes 140 hp. In 2001, the 146-hp BP-Z3 powerplant upped the ante with variable valve timing. At that time, Mazda also began offering 6-speed transmissions and big-brake upgrades. However, it wasn't until 2004 that Mazda introduced the first turbocharged Miata—the Mazdaspeed MX-5. With 178 hp, the BPT engine made the Mazdaspeed MX-5 the most powerful Miata ever.

The third-generation Miata is also now available. This Miata is based on an RX-8 chassis and comes with a 2.0L, 16-valve, 4-cylinder engine that produces 170 hp and is mated to a 5- or available 6-speed manual transmission. And you thought the Miata was for college girls.

Ford Mustang

Up to this point, I might have made it sound like the only cars you can drift are imports. That, however, is not the case. American muscle

Tire-smoking torque is one of the things that makes domestic muscle cars great for drifting. Although domestics weren't very popular in the early days of American drifting, it only took a few pioneers like Rhys Millen in his Pontiac GTO and Ken Gushi in his Ford Mustang to sway popular opinion. When drifting came to the States, it was only logical that drifters would begin to incorporate some of the vehicles that were readily available. Sure there are a good number of performance-minded Nissans and Toyotas here in the U.S., but there are far more Chevy, Ford, Pontiac, and other domestic muscle cars to choose from. (Ford Motor Company)

cars with eight or more cylinders are making their way into drifting competition, and the most popular domestic is the Ford Mustang. This is a logical progression for drifting here in the States. There is a finite number of high-performance RWD import cars available here, and most of them are older. New RWD imports are the minority and can be a little pricey. Not only are domestic, RWD cars like the Mustang readily available and relatively affordable, there are numerous performance parts available for them.

In 2005, the latest incarnation of the pony car was released and you can pick one up from your local Ford dealer starting at under 20K—of course that would be a V-6

model with 200 hp and 235 ft/lbs of torque. Those of you in the drifting community who have your eye on a Mustang will most likely step up to the GT, which comes standard with a 4.6L, 300-hp, SOHC V-8 coupled to a Tremec 5-speed manual transmission. Along with all that horsepower, this Mustang produces a whopping 320 ft/lbs of torque! The Mustang's power gets to the tires via Ford's trusty 8.8-inch solid rear axle, complete with 3.55:1 gears and Traction-Lok limited-slip differential. This gives drifters the ability to break their rear tires loose on command and keep them smoking around every corner of the track. The Mustang has a McPherson front suspension and a 3-link rear

suspension complete with coil springs and a Panhard rod. The car also comes with 4-wheel anti-lock disc brakes and a traction-control system. Where drifting is concerned, the new Mustang is pretty well equipped. With a little effort you can drift it, right off the lot. Of course, with a few upgrades it can be a competitive drift car.

Unfortunately, a new Mustang plus high-performance upgrades may be a little pricey for the first-time and even experienced drifter. But with a corral full of pre-owned Mustangs to choose from, there's definitely one for every budget. On top of availability and affordability, there are also plenty of aftermarket performance parts for them—there should be, considering the Mustang has been part of Ford's stable since 1964. The 1999–2004 Mustang GT came with a 260-hp, 4.6L, V-8 and a standard 5-speed transmission. These were the last of the Mustangs to utilize Ford's basic unibody Fox platform (aka: Fox-bodies), which dates back to 1979. Fox-bodies come with a McPherson strut front suspension and a four-link suspension and a solid axle in the rear. However, the '99, '01, '03, and '04 Mustang Cobras feature an independent rear suspension that is just as upgradeable. On top of that, '99 and '01 Cobras come with a 4.6L, DOHC, 32-valve, V-8 that puts out 320 hp. If you can afford it, '03 and '04 Cobras come with a supercharged 390-hp engine and T-56 6-speed transmission. All Cobras come with upgraded brakes, including 13-inch front discs with dual-piston calipers.

If you want to spend a little less money, check out a '94 to '98 Mustang. These Mustangs feature a smoother look than later Mustangs and a little less power, but much of

These new Ford Mustangs have done away with the Fox chassis that has been around in some form since 1979. Along with gobs of horsepower and torque available from the new 3-valve 4.6L V-8 engine, they have a MacPherson strut front suspension, and four-wheel-disc brakes. The Mustang's only real drawback is its solid rear axle, but it really isn't that big of a problem. (Ford Motor Company)

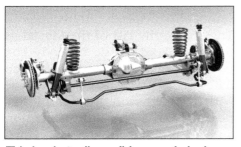

This is what a live solid rear axle looks like. If your car doesn't have independent rear suspension (IRS), it will have something like this. The rigid axle is part of the suspension, and older vehicles, as well as new trucks, use it for its simplicity and durability. 2005 and newer Mustangs use a 3-link design—two lower control arms and one upper control arm, and a Panhard bar to attach the rear end to the chassis and allow it to articulate. A Panhard rod (the bar running from left to right between the axle and sway bar) keeps the axle centered while allowing it travel up and down. IRS may be superior to the live axle for road racing, but the live axle will work just fine for drifting. (Ford Motor Company)

As if the immense amount of torque found stock in domestic V-8 powerplants wasn't enough, muscle cars are regularly supercharged for good measure. This Mustang features a Paxton centrifugal supercharger. There is an old rule of thumb for power that basically states: "More air in, more air out, more horsepower." There is some truth to this, but today's precision, electronically-controlled engines must also be properly tuned to make the best use of any changes from stock. (Travis Thompson)

everything else was the same. The '94–'95 GT came with a 215-hp 5.0L, while the '96–'98 GT came with a 4.6L SOHC V-8, still rated at 215 hp. In '94 and '95, the Mustang Cobra featured a 240-hp version of the 5.0L, but the '96 –'98 Cobra was blessed with an all-aluminum, DOHC, 32-valve, 4.6L V-8 that puts out 305 hp. Cobras also received upgraded brakes with 13-inch discs and dual-piston calipers up front. If you're into a really boxy look, check out an '82–'93 Mustang 5.0L GT, or an LX with the optional 5.0L V-8. By '86, these 5.0L Mustangs also came with T-5 5-speed manual transmission, the durable 8.8-inch rear end, and Trac-tion-Lok limited-slip differential.

There is no doubt that the Mustang has a long, detailed history. To find out more about late-model Mustangs that would make great drift cars, check out *High-Performance Mustang Buyer's Guide: 1979–Present*, by

The Mustang has a history in racing that dates back to the '60s, and it has always had plenty of available aftermarket performance parts. This also means there is a lot of information available on how to increase your Mustang's horsepower and maximize its handling, no matter what model year you're talking about. (Ford Motor Company)

If money is an issue, and it always is to some extent, then maybe an older Mustang will be your best option. There have been 300+ hp Cobras available since 1996, and 215-hp 5.0L Mustangs from the mid 1980s all the way to 1995.

Below: If you have any doubts about the Mustang, or any domestic car's ability to drift, then you need to see Ken Gushi in action. Even though he's still a teenager, he can keep up with professional racecar drivers like Samuel Hubinette in the Viper. Certainly this has a lot to do with his skill as a driver. But, skill alone isn't enough—even Ken needs a good car with the proper setup to drift like he does. Ken's Mustang has been gutted of all extraneous weight, the suspension was swapped out for a fully tunable setup, and a supercharger was added to its V-8 for even more horsepower and torque.

Travis Thompson. It goes into more detail than I could give here. In general, look for the Mustang in the best possible shape, with the highest-horsepower V-8, preferably with fuel injection and four-wheel disc brakes. If for some reason you wind up with something other than that, you still have options. The Mustang is blessed with a huge selection of aftermarket parts, as well as many factory upgrades and replacement parts available in your local salvage yard.

So Which Car is Best for You?

It always comes down to this question: Which is the best one for me? Of course, you are the only person who can answer that one, especially when it comes to a drift car. Certainly there are cars that you just happen to like more than others, which will help you narrow down the list. As I said in the beginning, "Any RWD vehicle with sufficient power for its weight is a possible candidate for a drift vehicle—it just depends on what you're comfortable with." This book was

not written to tell you which cars can be drifted and which can't. Instead, the idea is to show you some of the more popular vehicles and break them down into the various elements that make up a good drift car so you know what to look for in any vehicle.

Above, I only listed a handful of cars, but there are many more out there to choose from. Being in this list does not necessarily make them the best cars for drifting, either. I chose the cars on this list based on their popularity at drifting events, their availability in the U.S., and their price.

My goal is to show you the common elements that make any vehicle a good choice for drifting. These elements are handling, power-to-weight ratio, availability of performance parts, overall affordability, and local availability of the vehicle itself. Sure, you could import a Nissan Skyline or Toyota Chaser, which are popular drift cars in Japan. Over there these cars are relatively affordable, readily available, and there are plenty of performance parts for them. However, importing these cars and parts to the U.S. is expensive. So

why not focus on cars we already have here ready to go?

Elements of a Drift Car

What follows is a breakdown of the various elements that you need in a good drift car. Some of these are a given. Every car has a chassis and suspension—but that doesn't mean they're ideal for drifting. Most vehicles can benefit from some performance upgrades that make drifting easier. You can drift a stock, rear-wheel-drive car that has a sufficient power-to-weight ratio. But a car set up with the following elements, assuming they're all tuned properly, would be much easier to drift. When you search for your first drift car, keep these elements in mind and find a car that has as many of them as possible, or one that can easily and affordably be modified to include them.

Adjustable Suspension

If the drift car you choose only has one of the elements on this list—make sure it's good suspension. A fully tunable, four-wheel independent suspension is ideal, but a live

Can you drift Mom's old Volvo? That just depends on how creative you are. The crew at Kaplhenke Racing (www.kaplhenke.com) has outfitted their 240 series Volvo with various aftermarket parts and some custom pieces they offer to the public. This humble Volvo has 9.8:1 compression in its 2.3L inline four-cylinder engine—but the turbo produces 16 psi, helping it make 260 hp at the rear wheels. Kaplhenke Racing totally redesigned the front suspension including custom control arms and camber plates that allow for extra steering angle and a better alignment. It also has Koni DA struts and shocks adapted to fit the Volvo, with adjustable mounts made by Kaplhenke. For this competition, the crew also swapped in a welded factory differential. (UrbanRacer.com)

Alex Pfeiffer, one of the top drifters in the country, drives this S2000. This is the only new rear-wheel-drive car available from Honda (there's the NSX, but in the U.S. it's sold under the Acura name). There is nothing really bad to say about the S2000 for drifting except that at just over $34,000 for a new one, it's a little pricey.

(solid) rear axle and tunable independent front suspension will work. You want your suspension to be as adjustable as possible. You want adjustable ride height, damping, caster, camber, toe—even your sway bars should be adjustable. Various suspension upgrades on specific vehicles allow for adjustment of any or all of these variables where there was no factory adjustment.

Suspension adjustment is important so you can properly set up your car for drifting. Cars come from the factory set up to grip the road–not drift, so you'll need to tune it to achieve what you want.

Upgrading to fully adjustable coilovers with pillow-ball mounts that allow for increased camber adjustment is almost a necessity.

You can also use coilovers to adjust corner balance. You want a little more weight on the front so that the car will oversteer. A drift car's suspension should also be stiff enough to reduce body roll, but slightly more compliant in front to allow the front tires to follow the contour of the track and maintain more traction than the rear tires. You can achieve this with a softer setting on the front sway bar and dampers. Slightly less air pressure in the front tires will increase their contact patches and give them more grip as well.

Conversely, a stiffer, less-compliant rear suspension setup will make the rear tires easier to break loose, as will increased rear tire pressure for a smaller contact

patch. You can stiffen the rear by adding a larger-diameter and/or adjustable rear sway bar. Stiffer rear springs and dampers will also keep the rear end tight and contribute to oversteer. As you can see, your suspension has a lot of variables and is your link between the car and the track. It should be obvious how important it is for you to understand it all and know how to tune your suspension to achieve your desired result.

Increased Steering Angle

The further you can turn the wheels of your drift car, the better. The idea in drifting is to achieve the greatest slip angle possible without spinning out. To achieve maximum slip angle in competition, many pro-level drivers increase the steering angle of their car. Basically, this means they move the steering rack, change the steering rack, and/or install extended inner tie-rod ends to make their front wheels turn further in each direction than they could from the factory. This provides greater countersteering ability, which will allow you to maintain a drift with more slip angle than you could with a stock steering angle. Obviously, the more steering angle your car has stock, the better off you'll be.

Rigid Chassis

More is not always better, unless you are talking about chassis rigidity. Drifting puts stress on your car, and if your chassis is bending and twisting, the parts you install and set up for drifting won't be able to do their job properly. For example, it doesn't do you much good to fine-tune your alignment settings and suspension geometry if the unibody flexes and changes these settings while drifting.

Many of the more popular cars found at drifting events are based on unibody chassis. These are not usually as rigid as cars that have a body mounted to a separate frame, but that doesn't mean there's nothing you can do about it. Professional-level drift cars are typically seam-welded. This means that instead of the few spaced-out spot welds to hold the formed sheet metal sections of a unibody car together, drifters tack weld every place where sheet metal is joined along the length of the seam. Seam welding an entire car requires it to be stripped to the unibody shell, mounted in a jig to keep it aligned properly, and thousands of tack welds to be made, one right next to the other, without warping the metal. This process will make a chassis far more rigid, but auto manufacturers don't do it because it would cost a fortune and they want the car to flex slightly for a more comfortable ride. Seam welding your car is an expensive endeavor, and not a prerequisite of drifting, but it couldn't hurt.

If you're building a serious drift car, you should also install a roll cage. It's easiest to install one when you have your car stripped to do the seam welding. A cage will stiffen up even a fully seam

Like many popular drift cars, the RX-8 is built on a unibody chassis. It is made up of numerous sheetmetal panels that are stamped into shape and then welded together. The individual pieces bend and flex easily, but when they're all welded together, the chassis as whole becomes relatively rigid. Manufacturers space out spot welds along each seam or joint to hold these pieces together, while still providing a small amount of flex to soak up bumps and vibration for a more comfortable ride. This is good for the average consumer, but the chassis should be rigid for the best possible performance. To make a chassis more rigid you can add welds along each seam, which requires the car to be stripped down almost to the point of this rendering. (Mazda)

If you want to drift an American muscle car, you can also check out the Chevrolet Camaro and Pontiac Trans Am. Buying an older car like this will certainly mean that the engine and other parts may be tired from all the miles. Luckily, it is easy to install a new, more powerful crate motor in place of a tired V-8 or even the V-6 found in these cars. Other suspension, brake, and drivetrain upgrades are just as affordable and easy to find. The result is a reliable, tire-smoking drifter.

welded car, plus it protects you in the event of a crash.

If you're just getting started or you're building a street/drift car, strut tower bars are an affordable way to stiffen things up. Vehicle-specific strut tower bars are readily available for most vehicles mentioned above and they're usually quite easy to install. Strut tower bars are great for drifting because they help your suspension geometry stay consistent even during a high-speed drift. Subframe connectors or other chassis braces are also available for some cars. Subframe connectors do just what they claim: they connect the front and rear subframe, adding strength and rigidity, mimicking a traditional frame. Mustang drag and road racers have sworn by these for years, and they are just as applicable to building a sturdy drift car.

Increased Horsepower

No, you don't need the most powerful car in the world to drift. Typical drift cars range from 200 to 700 hp, but in fact, drifting is one motorsport where too much power can be a bad thing. The minimum power you need to drift is whatever it takes to break your rear wheels loose on command and maintain wheel spin throughout a turn, and this mystical power level is different for every car. You don't want so much power that you lose control and spin out while trying to maintain a drift.

There is a reason that there aren't any power classes in drifting competition—a relatively low-powered AE86 Corolla can not only compete with, but even beat a Dodge Viper in a drifting competition. All other factors being equal, the power required to drift is relative to the weight of the vehicle—the heavier the car gets, the more power it'll need to drift. However, a car can be too heavy for drifting. Ideally, you want the lightest car possible with the appropriate power. Smaller, lightweight imports like the S13 or AE86 can get by with as little as 200 hp, while slightly heavier domestic muscle cars benefit from their more torquey V-8 engines with 300 hp to 500 hp. More power in the smaller cars wouldn't hurt, but anything less in the bigger, heavier domestic muscle and drifting consistently would be more difficult. Another way to think of it is that you want the most reliable horsepower you can get from a given engine. Don't forget the other part of the power-to-weight ratio—lightening your car is just like adding extra horsepower—except it's a lot cheaper.

How you achieve the horsepower you need depends on your taste and your budget. It is possible to drift with a stock engine. Typically even stock drift cars have minimal bolt-on performance parts to increase horsepower. Forced induction is a popular method of adding horsepower whether it is a turbo or supercharger. Programmable engine management systems are also a great way to fine-tune your car's performance. Regardless of how you do it, you need to make sure your drift car has the power necessary to keep the rear tires spinning.

You also need to make sure you set up your engine so that it is not prone to overheating. Drift cars run extremely hot because of the power it takes to keep the rear tires spinning, and airflow across the radiator and engine is not ideal when the car is sliding sideways.

Upgraded Brakes

It goes without saying that brakes are important, but that doesn't mean you need the biggest set of brakes available for your car. Although larger-diameter brake rotors do offer increased braking performance, they also increase rotational mass, effec-

tively slowing your car down when you're not on the brakes, though the effect is minimal. Big brakes do have advantages to drifting, however, and how big you go should depend on your braking needs. At the very least, you want four-wheel-disc brakes—drum brakes don't work nearly as well. Even better is to have vented and slotted rotors. Many think that these upgrades are for cooling, but in actuality they are designed to allow gases generated from the pads, when they get hot, to escape. These gases lubricate the pads and don't allow them to grip the rotor as well as they could otherwise, so it's important to give these gases a place to go. Up from

there you have larger vented, slotted, and cross-drilled rotors and/or four or more piston calipers. Larger rotors will offer increased braking, and their increased size helps dissipate heat. Basically you should install the biggest brakes you need, not the biggest brakes you can buy.

Possibly even more important than the increased braking performance (assuming your car performs well in that department) is avoiding brake fade. Brake fade can be caused by the brake fluid boiling or by the rotors and pads heating up, which will decrease their efficiency. You can tell when your brakes fade, because you won't be able to slow the car as effectively and the brake pedal will feel soft and spongy. Brake fade occurs during prolonged or excessive braking, so you can resolve the problem by easing off the brakes. Of course, that will limit how fast and how hard you drive and is probably a sign that you need to upgrade your brakes.

One word of warning: In many cases, cars with four-wheel-disc brakes have drum brakes in the center of the rear rotors that are used for the e-brake. Avoid this setup if you can because the e-brake is an important part of drifting so it should perform at the same level as your regular brakes. Ideally your e-brake lever will be a direct link to your rear calipers.

Limited-Slip Differential (LSD)

To LSD, or not to LSD, is that really the question? Although you can start drifting without an LSD, this is the pro's rear-end setup of choice. By distributing power to both of the rear wheels, the LSD makes breaking them both loose much easier. Without the LSD (known as an open differential), it's possible for just one wheel to spin

Look for a drift car with good brakes from the factory and you may not have to upgrade. Mustang Cobras from 1994–2004 came with 13-inch rotors and dual-piston calipers up front. (Travis Thompson)

while the other grips. This makes initiating a drift more unpredictable and difficult.

You can find a car that comes from the factory with a limited-slip differential, install a factory LSD in place of your open differential, or you can buy an aftermarket unit. Aftermarket LSDs can be set up to lock at different rates from 50 percent to 100 percent based on the number and type of friction clutches inside.

One-hundred percent lock means the rear wheels are virtually locked together; anything less than that refers to how much one wheel can slip, or rotate, in relation to the other. A lot of times, people who also drive their drift cars on the street will set their LSD up to lock at around 80 percent, which still allows them to break their tires loose on demand. This setup also allows the rear wheels to move more

independently around a turn and isn't as aggressive for street driving as a fully locked-up differential, which can cause loss of control in certain conditions like rain or snow. Differentials with a high lock-up percentage can be noisy and difficult to maneuver around tight corners when you're not drifting.

You can always start out with whatever differential your car comes with and move up to an aftermarket LSD as your skills progress. The trick is making sure there's an LSD available for the vehicle you plan to drift before you buy it. And, if you're starting out with an LSD that has a high percentage of lock, it's a good idea to practice driving it in a safe place until you get used to it. If you have an aftermarket LSD, it's a good idea to start out with a lower percentage of lock. Of course, to change the percentage of lock in your differ-

ential you have to take apart the entire unit and rebuild it to your desired specs.

Comfort and Safety

Whatever car you choose for drifting should be set up to be comfortable. I'm not talking about leaning the seat back and draping one arm over the steering wheel. In a drift car, or any type of racecar for that matter, you need to be properly strapped into a race seat that has large side bolsters for lateral support and fits your frame. That seat should be covered in a material that won't allow you to slide around, and it should position you so that your arms are bent at about 90 degrees when gripping the steering wheel. Your knees should also be slightly bent so you have access to the full travel of the gas, brake, and clutch pedals. A secure 5-point

Budgets are all relative. You, for example, may be able to afford a Porsche for drifting. As you can see, this 911 Carrera 2 has no problem getting sideways. (Antony Fraser)

harness is also a must, as long as the car is equipped with a roll cage. This is because a 4- or 5-point harness will hold you and your head securely in place. The roll cage is required to protect you and your head in case of a roll over.

The right seat and a good harness, or at least a good seat belt, will help hold you in place and allow you to focus on driving rather than keeping your body from moving around. A more solid racing seat with less padding and solid frame securing it to the chassis will also transmit valuable information about the track and your car.

The same can be said about the steering wheel. It will transmit information to your hands that will help you better understand what's happening with the track and the car. I recommend a quality aftermarket steering wheel with a continuous round hoop—because you'll be using every inch of it when drifting.

Your shifter should be easy to access quickly, as should all three control pedals. You don't want a shifter with a loose or slippery shift knob that's too far out of reach, or big aftermarket pedal covers that interfere with your ability to use the clutch, brake, or throttle.

What to Avoid

For the most part, this book has been written with a budget in mind, and I feel there's no reason to spend more money on a drift car than you need to. Certainly, there are people out there who could afford to buy a new Porsche or NSX for a drift car, but cars like this are not only expensive to purchase, but costly to maintain. Drifting takes a lot out of a car, so you want to choose something that you can afford to get parts for. It's important

to be realistic about your goals and your funds. It's no fun having a half-built car that you can't afford to finish. I actually spent just $425 on my drift car. Of course, I had to spend a lot more to set it up properly, but I didn't spend anywhere near the $30K that some new, stock drift cars cost. Why spend the money if you don't have to?

Speaking of the budget, another thing that might not be in your best interest is huge wheels and tires. I know big wheels are all the rage, but there's a limit to how big your wheels should be on a drift car, or any performance car for that matter. The largest wheel I would choose is an 18. You could probably get away with a 19, but anything bigger is just about the bling. Larger wheels not only increase rotational mass, but have to be built heavier overall to keep from falling apart. Larger wheels allow you to run a lower-profile tire with less sidewall for decreased body roll, which is great, but as the tire size increases, so does the cost.

Here again, I chose to save some money on my drift car and went with 17-inch wheels. I made the tradeoff to have slightly more sidewall in my tires, although less than stock, in favor of more affordable tires. If I only had to buy one set of tires it wouldn't have been that big of a deal, but knowing that I can easily go through a set of tires in one day, I opted for the more affordable rubber.

One more thing you need to be aware of when choosing tires is their speed rating. Most of the 18- and 19-inch tires only come in a super-sticky compound, which will be much harder to break loose—remember that these are performance tires designed to grip. Instead, you should consider slightly harder tires, which are readily available in smaller tire sizes.

You don't want a heavy car either. The heavier a car is, the harder it will be to manage when drifting. It's harder to initiate a drift with a heavier car, and harder to maintain

"You can not drift a big, heavy, 4-door sedan." Obviously, Ken Nomura has proven that statement incorrect. Remember: You can make anything with four wheels oversteer. The funny thing is that a lot of the newer sports cars in this list weigh in at 3,300 to 3,500lbs, which is pretty heavy. The factory curb weight of an ER-34 Skyline is around 3,000 lbs, but Ken's Skyline was lightened to a mere 2,640 lbs!

With a 500 hp 8.3L V-10 engine, the Dodge Viper is the most powerful car in this chapter, and at over $85K, it's also the most expensive. Samuel Hubinette pilots the Mopar Performance Dodge Viper in competition and it's no wonder they chose an accomplished racecar driver to get the job done. Although you probably wouldn't have to do anything to a Viper to make it drift right off the show-room floor, I can't recommend this as a drift car for the beginner.

the drift without spinning out. You also need more power to drift a heavy car and you will have to drive it harder and faster to get it to drift. Even though you see them at drift events, many consider the Toyota Supra to be a heavy car for drifting. Of course, you can make plenty of power with a Supra and lighten it up by removing the interior, sound deadening, and various other luxury accoutrements. Basically you want to keep this in mind when looking for your drift car and if you find one that you feel is a little too heavy, figure out what you can do to lighten it up before you buy it.

Mid-engine cars are not ideal for drifting. Certainly you can drift an NSX or MR2, but it's very different than a typical front-engine car. The reason is mid-engine cars are too well balanced. To drift them, the driver must constantly shift weight onto the front end to get them to oversteer rather than understeer.

Finally, and most importantly, you don't want a car that you can't get stock and aftermarket parts for. Even if you can find an incredible deal on a lightweight, high-performance car, it won't be a bargain if you can't get parts for it. Even cars that do have readily available stock parts aren't a good idea if no aftermarket manufacturer makes high-performance upgrades for them. Sure, you could make custom parts, but that would be expensive and time consuming. When you narrow down your search to one car, start researching aftermarket parts availability before you buy it.

If you can't find the stuff you need to make it a drift car, at reasonable prices, move on to your next choice.

The bottom line when choosing a vehicle for drifting is to set a budget for both the vehicle and modifications, and then use that information to find a vehicle you like that will suit your needs. In competition, everything from Samuel Hubinette's Dodge Viper to Bubba Drift's LS1-equipped, automatic transmission El Camino have handled some extreme drifting situations. This goes to show you can drift just about anything on four wheels—if you have it set up properly and possess the necessary car- control skills. In the following chapter, I'll apply what you read here to the real-world build-up of an entry-level drift car.

BUILDING A DRIFT CAR

If you're serious about drifting and actually want to go out and do it, you'll need a drift car. Practicing in the family sedan just isn't a good idea, unless your mom happens to have a 240SX with a 5-speed—and isn't worried about its paint or tires.

When I committed to writing this book I immediately set out to find a good drift car to use when illustrating the how-to projects and car set-up. I put a lot of thought into choosing the car I felt was best for me to drift, and which would be representative of what most drifters are using. Depending on what you're looking for, you may have to put a lot of thought into what will be the right drift car for you. All of this

This is it: my dirty, dented, oxidized, weather-beaten 240SX. I picked it up from an apartment complex just outside of Vegas and am sure the people who lived there were happy to see it go. It doesn't look like much at this point, but this car was exactly what I needed. It was close enough for me to pick up and it was cheap—just $425 on eBay. I felt no reason to take more money out of my budget for cleaner car when most of what you see here was going to be replaced, including the hood, front fascia, wheels, and tires. As for the rest of the body, a few dents won't hinder my ability to drift, and because the car is already in this shape, I won't feel so bad when I add some damage of my own!

Under the hood was a KA24DE—well, most of it anyway. Even though I had no intention of using this powerplant, the fact that this was a '92 240SX, with a DOHC engine, would save time and money later on. The power-steering reservoir and throttle cable on this car both work with the SR20DET that will replace the KA. That would not be the case with an SOHC KA24E car.

The rest of the engine was in the trunk (did you think I was kidding?). It may seem like a good idea to throw out parts you think you don't need when building a car like this, but you should keep everything until the project is complete. You never know what you might need along the way or what you can sell to help offset your budget or subsidize more upgrades—someone on eBay needs that valve cover.

The interior had seen better days. It was sun-faded and marinated in soda—did I mention the car only cost $425? Seriously, this was no big deal for me, as I planned to gut the interior of this drift car from the start. These seats could have stayed; other than being a little dirty, they have decent side bolsters for stock seats, which will help hold you in place while you slide the car from side to side. When you're choosing a drift car, check out the stock seats. If they're supportive enough to get you by, use them when you first start out to save some money.

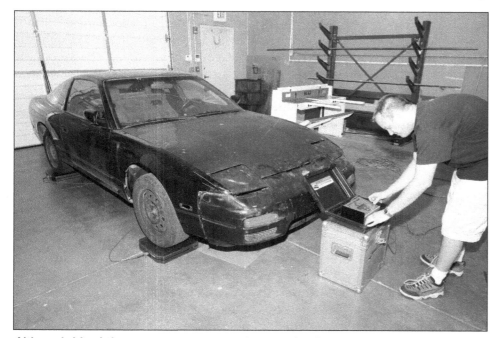

Although I had the strong urge to gut the car, the first thing I did was weigh it to find out the corner balance, and determine the stock weight before I got started. Luckily, my good friend Rob Benner had access to a set of computerized scales and brought them to Fesler Productions in Phoenix, where I did all the work on the car, which was an added bonus considering the car didn't run. Any shops in your area that build road-racing or autocross cars should be able to cornerweight your car for you.

What I found was that my car weighed in at 2,719 lbs and was very well balanced from one corner to the next. The front left weighed 689, the front right 764, rear left 669, and rear right 597. With just slightly more weight up front, the car will have a natural tendency to oversteer, which is just you want in drifting.

What you are looking at here is dead weight. If you're building a car specifically for drifting, various interior panels, rear seats, and carpet can be removed. You don't have to do this to drift, but it couldn't hurt. The only thing you need in a drift car is a dash (you need one to compete), door panels, and at least one good seat—the center console found its way back into this project as well. If you plan on turning your daily driver into a drifter, you can keep whatever you need.

After all was said and done, this is what my interior looked like. Depending on what your car has from the factory, you could go one step further and remove the sound deadening to lighten up the car even more. Besides gutting the interior, I removed the hood, front bumper, and fenders for access to every part of the car that I would be modifying. Once everything is put back together, I should have a lighter, faster, more rigid car that is ready to be dialed in for drifting.

depends on where you live and what the demand is for the increasingly popular drift cars in your area. As the popularity of drifting rises, and the number of the more-popular driftable cars decreases, their prices will certainly go up.

While perusing eBay for a candidate, I stumbled upon a '92 240SX with a blown KA24DE. The body was straight enough, and everything I would be keeping on the car was intact and in good condition. As it turns out, this 240 was handed down from mom to son before the engine submitted to the sweltering Las Vegas heat. Lucky for me, its owner was more into racing than drifting and offered up the car for under $500.

As I've mentioned, the 240SX, in this case the S13 chassis, is by far the most popular drift car around. This is thanks to its light weight, good corner balance, independent front and rear suspension, and its very desirable powerplant options, including the SR20DET. There are also plenty of aftermarket performance parts available for the 240.

Like many of the U.S. 240s, this one came with a naturally aspirated KA24DE, which I'd consider an added bonus regardless of the fact

that it was blown—you'll see why later. On the downside, this was also one of the many 240s that came with an automatic transmission. Although the KA24DE is a decent, affordable choice for drifting and it does have good aftermarket support, it's regularly swapped out for the ever-popular, turbocharged, intercooled, JDM SR20DET. Though the KA could have stayed, the automatic transmission had to go.

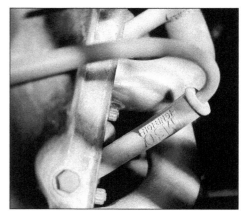

One of the first things your new drift car needs is a tune-up. Where possible, upgrade to heavy-duty or performance parts. You should replace your spark plugs and wires, and even your distributor cap and rotor if your car has them. Don't forget your fuel, oil, and air filters as well. (Travis Thompson)

Tune-Up and Maintenance

If you are new to drifting, you should find a car that runs well and has a manual transmission. It's a good idea to learn in a bone-stock car if at all possible. You need to get a feel for how a car handles and responds when you try to put it into a drift. You will break parts on your car as you learn to drift, so they might as well be stock parts that can be easily and cheaply replaced or upgraded to superior aftermarket parts when you're ready. As your skills progress and you start to understand how to better control your car, you can upgrade it to better suit your driving ability. Learning the various aspects of drifting in your stock car will help you choose the right upgrades for your driving style. It can also teach you how to set up and tune these parts.

Once you have your hands on your drift car of choice, go over the entire car and make sure it's in good working order. Check every nut and bolt to make sure they are properly tightened and replace anything on the engine, suspension, or brakes that is worn or damaged.

After that, you need to do a full tune-up and all the routine mainte-

These Gatorback belts were only a few dollars more than stock replacements, which should mean they are more durable and will last longer.

nance. Throw in some fresh spark plugs, wires, and a distributor cap and rotor (if your car has these). Don't forget a new air filter and fuel filter. You don't want your engine to miss, sputter or die as you attempt to drift because it will make the task that much more difficult. Change all the fluids, including the oil, radiator fluid, transmission fluid, and the differential gear oil. You also want to make sure all your belts are in good shape and that they are under the proper amount of tension.

Cooling may actually be the most important aspect of engine performance for drifting. Radiators, cooling fans, and the various vents that allow air into the engine bay are designed to cool your engine when the car is moving forward in a straight line. While drifting, your car is traveling at an angle, often under full power, so your engine is generating maximum heat and the elements designed to reduce this heat are not working at peak efficiency.

With that in mind, it's a good idea to flush your radiator and fill it with a mix of distilled water (this helps reduce corrosion within your cooling system) and a high-quality radiator fluid. There are also various coolant additives available at your local auto parts store that can increase the efficiency of the coolant—every little bit helps. Since most drift cars are at least a few years old, it might not be a bad idea to change your thermostat at the same time. The standard one from your local auto parts store will be fine, but choose one with a slightly lower opening temp as this will help keep things cool under the hood.

Once you've attended to the engine, it's time to go over the entire suspension system. Everyone seems to agree that the suspension is the most important system on a drift car.

First and foremost, you want your car to handle predictably, and that's impossible with old, worn out bushings and ball joints. These should all be replaced with, at the very least, new stock pieces from your local auto parts store.

While you're under the car, check all the suspension components such as the upper and lower control arms, struts and springs, sway bars, tie-rods, tension rods, and everything else.

If you happened to buy a car with springs that have been cut or heated (which is even worse) to lower it, replace them immediately. Springs that have been modified couldn't possibly have the proper spring rate, much less a consistent

If you can tell you need new ball joints by the slop in your suspension, they are really far gone. Even if you think your suspension feels solid, swapping out your old ball joints is a good idea. The one on the left didn't seem bad at all until it was removed from the car and the excess play became obvious. The new unit on the right is a stock, heavy-duty upgrade that is free from play and has a Zerk fitting incorporated so it can be greased as well (the stock ball joint was not serviceable). Due to the stress put on these parts when drifting, the ability to service them really is a necessity.

These are steering rack bushings from a 240SX. The one on the left is obviously stock, while the new one on the right is from Energy Suspension. Soft, broken-down, worn stock bushings will allow the suspension components to move around. Aftermarket bushings are typically much stiffer than even new, stock bushings and will greatly reduce any unnecessary movement and play, which means increased performance.

spring rate from left to right, which will make things very unpredictable when you attempt to transfer weight from one side of the car to the other in a drift. Use only unmodified stock or aftermarket performance springs. If you can compress your struts by hand, or push down on a corner of your car and compress the suspension easily, they are worn out and also need to be replaced.

Suspension may be the most important aspect of a drift car, but brakes are the most important part of any car for safety. It sucks if your car doesn't run, but that's far better than not being able to stop. You want to drain the brake fluid and replace it with fresh, clean brake fluid as recommended by your owner's manual. You may also need new brake pads and rotors. Once the brakes have been gone over and any worn or damaged parts have been replaced, fully bleed the brakes to make sure all the air is gone from the lines.

Stock wheels and tires are fine, even if the tires have some wear.

What you don't want are tires that are totally bald, dry rotted, hard, unevenly worn, or have bubbles or steel belts showing. Sure, you may end up with a blowout as you wear your tires down to nothing, but you don't want to start out drifting with tires that are too far gone. The fun will be over before it starts.

Like any motorsport, drifting is dangerous, and safety for yourself and others should be of the utmost importance. With that in mind, you need to make sure you are properly restrained in your vehicle when you drift. For an entry-level car, a factory bucket seat with decent side bolsters, like those that come stock in a 240, along with factory seat belts that are in good condition, will get you by.

Believe it or not, you do NOT want a 4- or 5-point harness unless you have a race-spec roll cage. You won't even pass tech inspection at a sanctioned racing or drifting event if you have racing harness without a roll cage, because in the case of a rollover, you would not be able to move your head. Even if your car is stock, a roll cage would offer up added safety and allow the proper use of a 4- or 5-point racing harness—this would be a smart place to spend the first money modifying your drift car.

Make sure everything works properly inside the car. Fix any loose carpet, floor mats, or interior panels that might get in your way. You also want to make sure your gas, brake, and clutch pedals don't have worn, slippery pads or cheap aftermarket pedal covers that could interfere with your driving. The e-brake should be properly adjusted, as you will use it to help initiate a drift and balance the car. The stock steering wheel will get you by in the beginning, as will the stock shift

knob, just make sure they're both in good condition. Ultimately, your car's interior and controls should be comfortable and reliable so you can focus on drifting. And finally, go out and invest in a good-quality helmet—you can never be too safe.

$10,000 Drift Car Build-Up

If you are dedicated and practice a lot with something similar to the aforementioned Level 1 drift car, chances are your drifting skills will improve. If you get this far, it's time to start upgrading your drift car so that it will allow you to drift harder, faster, and at a more aggressive angle of attack—this is what the $10K drift car build-up is all about. Practicing with your stock drift car will teach you which parts or systems you need to upgrade. At first you might just need a lower center of gravity and stiffer suspension to reduce body roll. Maybe you want a more rigid chassis—and you will no doubt want more power. You can upgrade as you go (or as you break stuff), or do it all in one shot. Only your skill level and budget can limit what you do to your car.

With this in mind, I set out with a bargain-basement 240SX, a very obtainable $10K budget, and the desire to build a car strictly for drifting. If a part doesn't make the car easier or safer to drift—you won't see it here. Why $10,000? Because that seems like a reasonable amount and it should be just enough to put together a respectable drift car.

On top of making this project financially obtainable, I also wanted to use parts that were easy to find. Right now, a segment of the U.S. drifting community is very biased toward imported cars and using very esoteric imported performance parts for them. There is nothing wrong with that. This 240 will have its fair share of imported parts and, of course, the car itself is imported. But there's no reason to spend a lot of extra money and wait long periods of time to get parts from the other side of the world when there are similar, more readily available parts right here in the U.S.

The only requirements for the parts I put on this car are that they: 1) make the car easier or safer to drift, 2) they are high quality, 3) they are readily available anywhere in the U.S., and 4) they are not prohibitively expensive. Though the installs shown apply directly to the Nissan 240SX, the principles and process can apply to whatever drift car you choose. After all, the most popular drift cars all share the same basic layout: front engine, rear drive, manual transmission. When you're deciding which drift car you'd like to start with, it's a good idea to research the available upgrades, including their cost and availability, and factor that into your buying decision. You might be surprised how much the price of a given upgrade can vary from car to car.

Since I knew I wanted to make the SR20DET swap, which typically involves purchasing a complete 240 front clip from Japan with everything from the engine and intercooler to the transmission and gauge cluster, it seemed obvious that a $500 car with an automatic transmission and a blown engine would be perfect for this swap. Like I said before, 240s typically go for around $2,000 in decent, running condition. Of course, there's no reason to spend the money on a car that runs just to pull its engine out and discard it. Because this engine swap is pretty involved, I dedicated an entire chapter to it. To see what I

went through to put an SR20DET in my drift car, check out Chapter 6.

As for the rest of the car, this chapter shows everything I did and what aftermarket parts I used to make my 240SX the best drift car it could be for the money. Check it out.

Suspension and Brake Upgrades

Suspension is the most important aspect of a drift car, so I decided to start there and put the majority of my budget into suspension upgrades. Drift cars can benefit from a number of suspension upgrades, but I'm going to concentrate on adjustable coil-overs, strut tower braces, sway bars, and stiffer, more durable bushings. Depending on which drift car you start out with, there may also be control arms, tension rods, lateral rods, and various other suspension components available.

The point of any of these mods is to help you drift. They do this by adding adjustability so you can better set up the car to oversteer, keeping your alignment settings consistent, and by reducing slop in the factory suspension—these elements will make it easier to break the rear tires loose when initiating a drift, or keep the car balanced to maintain a drift.

Adjustable coil-overs are extremely important as they give drifters and racers the ability to set up their car so that they can more easily achieve their goal. Coil-overs are just that; a coil mounted over the shock absorber. Specifically, coil-overs have threaded bodies so, at the very least, spring preload can be adjusted, which will allow you some corner balance adjustment. In some cases, as with the JIC-Magic coil-overs, the spring perch is also adjustable so you can fine-tune ride height. High-end coil-overs can also include camber plates or pillow ball mounts that allow for added adjust-

This is JIC Magic's flagship FLT-A2 coil-over setup ($1,850 retail, paid $1,630). These coil-overs feature 15-way adjustable monotube nitrogen gas dampers, ride height adjustment that is independent of spring perch adjustment, and upper pillow ball mounts that allow for camber adjustment. JIC Magic offers FLT-A2 coil-overs for various other cars as well. If they don't make a set of coil-overs for your drift car, there is very likely a manufacturer that does.

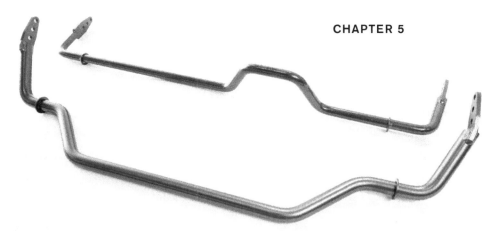

These JIC Magic control arms ($279) replace the factory units with their sloppy rubber bushings and allow rear toe adjustment to improve traction and stability. As you can see, their length is adjustable and they feature solid spherical bearings. Depending on what type of rear suspension your car has, manufacturers may offer control arms like this for your application. If not, you can at least upgrade the bushings in your stock control arms with stiffer polyurethane bushings.

Upgraded sway bars, or anti-roll bars as The Progress Group calls them, were next on my list. Aftermarket bars like these are much heftier than their factory counterparts, and they're often adjustable as well. These even come with precision Heim joint end links to replace the relatively sloppy factory units with rubber bushings. I picked this set up for $430. Depending on what drift car you have, there may or may not be an adjustable set available.

ment of camber and caster. And, finally, many high-end coil-overs also come with adjustable dampers, which allow you to adjust the stiffness of each independently.

With a regular coil spring and damper setup (strut, or MacPherson Strut), you will not have any of the adjustments found in even the most basic coil-over. You can, however, swap in stiffer and/or shorter coil springs, as well as adjustable

dampers, but you're pretty much stuck with one particular ride height once you get them installed. How you set up and tune your suspension will depend on your particular car and your driving style.

In general you want to set up your car with slightly more weight up front, and have a more compliant suspension setup in front than in the rear. This will allow the front tires to better follow the contour of the track for maximum traction while doing the opposite in the rear. You can also dial in a degree or two of negative camber up front to increase the outside front tire's contact patch during heavy cornering. How you set up each of these variables will depend on you and your specific car. Ideally, beginners should start with fairly neutral settings and put in as much track time as possible to adjust them and see how each affects their drifting.

When shopping for coil-overs, you'll need to rely on someone with experience in racing or drifting. You can ask around, but often the coil-over manufacturer will have good recommendations of where to start as far as spring rates, spring heights,

and damping for your particular car are concerned. For this reason, it is a good idea to research the suspension companies that are prevalent in drifting. JIC-Magic, Kei-Office, Tanabe, Tein, and others are heavily involved in the sport, and many offer drift-specific coil-over systems. This isn't to say these are the only companies to use, but you want to do your homework and make sure the coil-overs you buy are suitable for drifting.

If coil-overs are too pricey for you to start out with, consider a set of lowered performance springs over a good set of struts with adjustable dampers. Maximum adjustment is ideal, but you can get by with a lower center of gravity, and relatively stiff and predictable set of springs.

Adding a set of front and rear strut tower bars will stiffen up your chassis. They help reduce flex between the left and right strut tow-

This set of CS-2 strut tower bars from DC Sports ($165 each) features a dual bar design with an integrated steel brace to eliminate body flex for improved handling. If you're planning an engine swap, make sure the front bar will work with your new engine. Strut tower bars, some of better quality than others, are available for most if not all of the cars you would consider for drifting.

These JIC Magic inner tie-rod ends ($175) feature thicker shafts than the stock units and they are said to allow for a tighter steering radius. JIC Magic also offers other upgrades for the S13, including Rear Traction Rods, Pillow Tension Rods, and Rear Camber Adjustable Upper Arms.

Any upgraded suspension components you buy should come with new, upgraded bushings, and it would simply be wrong to leave the rest of the worn out, sloppy factory rubber bushings in place. Energy Suspension offers their HYPER-FLEX SYSTEM of polyurethane bushings in a Master Bushing Set ($140 for the S13). All the rigid polyurethane bushings, insert sleeves, and grease you need to replace every suspension bushing in the car is included. The 240SX kit includes rear subframe inserts and steering rack bushings, as well. It won't be hard to find who offers individual bushings, as well as complete bushing kits, for your drift car.

ers, which will keep your alignment settings consistent, even under harsh drifting conditions. They are available for just about every car on the road, but they aren't all created equal. When you're shopping for strut tower bars, look for a sturdy set. The best models feature a solid, one-piece design that doesn't have any joints to allow flex.

Aftermarket sway bars are a popular upgrade for drifters and racers alike. Thicker aftermarket bars offer increased stiffness, which will help decrease body roll. Any decent sway bar set should also come with new polyurethane bushings for less slop, but you may have to order new end links, complete with poly bushings, separately. Some aftermarket sway bars also offer adjustment by way of multiple mounting positions for the end links. The further in the end links are mounted, the stiffer the sway bar will be. Conversely, the further out, the more compliant it will be.

Depending on which drift car you're building, there may also be various other suspension components available. Depending on their function and cost, they may or may not be worth adding to your drift car, at least in the beginning. I have tried to list the bare minimum necessary to start out drifting. And

remember that you can drift a totally stock car. Any additional aftermarket parts should only be added as you need them. You might need to upgrade a control arm or link bar for added strength, to reduce slop, or to add adjustment where there was none from the factory. Regardless of the reason, you should only swap out stock parts for aftermarket parts when you actually have a reason, not just because the parts look cool.

I mentioned replacing bushings in the first part of this chapter, and you should at the very least replace old, worn bushing with new, stock pieces. Even better is to upgrade to stiffer, polyurethane bushings that keep your suspension components properly aligned so they only move in their intended direction. This means consistent caster and camber alignment throughout the suspension travel and ultimately better, more predictable acceleration, cornering, and braking performance, whether you're racing or drifting.

Many aftermarket suspension components come with stiffer bush-

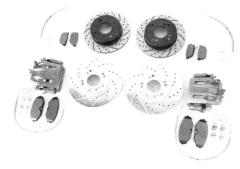

Fast Brakes offers three different upgrades for the 240, and I chose their middle-of-the-road setup for around $700. The kit includes Infinity Q45 rotors and calipers with high performance pads for the front and a rotor/pad upgrade for the rear. When upgrading the brakes on any car, choose the right size for your needs, not simply the largest that are available.

ings or even solid bearings, but you shouldn't overlook the stock bushings that are left behind on components that you didn't upgrade. You can order individual poly bushings for them or even complete kits from companies like Energy Suspension or Prothane. Bushing kits are a great, affordable upgrade even if you're

For my 240, I chose a set of 17 x 7.5-inch Konig Hurry wheels and Falken Azenis 215/40R17 tires. The wheels are lightweight, look good, and just the right size for this entry-level car. I will also be keeping the stock, 15-inch steel wheels and outfitting them with a similar set of Falken tires as backups-this is just another reason to go with the relatively small Fast Brakes big brake upgrade. The complete wheel and tire package set me back just under $800-you can spend that much on a single 18-inch wheel!

Tires are extremely important for drifting, and anyone into the sport, even at an amateur level, will be going through plenty of them. First off, there is no one perfect tire for drifting, and you don't need 19-inch tires with super sticky rubber compounds. In fact, you want a slightly harder tire, especially in the rear, that will be somewhat easier to break loose. This doesn't mean you want old, hard, dry tires that won't grip the asphalt at all. You want tires that can be broken loose in a turn and yet will still grip the track enough for you to control the car and maintain your drift. Falken not only offers a variety of performance tires in various sizes, but they are heavily involved in drifting and were one of the companies instrumental in bringing the sport to the U.S early on. (Falken)

sticking with mostly stock components—you'll definitely feel the difference.

Braking is important on any vehicle, but when you increase horsepower and handling performance, increased braking performance is even more important. For many, this means slapping the biggest, most expensive brakes they can find under a set of huge wheels. If you're on a budget, there's no need to step up to 18-inch or larger wheels, on top of paying for huge brakes.

You should upgrade your brakes to suit your needs, not your car's appearance. If you're running a relatively stock engine with moderate horsepower, and your car already has decent four-wheel-disc brakes, you may be able to get by with a pad upgrade. Beyond that, you should increase the size of your rotors and possibly install a set of 2- or 4-piston calipers. Aftermarket brake setups with larger rotors (more friction surface area) and multi-piston calipers

give you increased braking performance, and they offer more consistent performance on longer runs where heat buildup and brake fade would otherwise diminish braking performance.

Upgrading to braided stainless steel brake lines is a worthwhile investment, especially since they're relatively cheap. This is even more true if your old lines are dry and worn. Braided lines don't expand or bulge under pressure like rubber lines and thus provide a more solid pedal feel. This makes it easier to use your brakes when drifting as you will receive more accurate feedback through the brake pedal and be able to more easily respond with precise brake input.

As for wheels and tires, drifting doesn't require the largest set of wheels available. If you want, you can drift on stock 14-inch rims and tires. If your car comes with stock 14- or 15-inch wheels it is certainly a good idea to keep them as spares. Depending on what car you're

starting with, there may be factory 16- or 17-inch wheels available that would make a great budget upgrade.

Whether stock or aftermarket, I suggest wheels that are fairly lightweight and affordable, with a set of high-quality tires that aren't too sticky. The benefit to larger 17- or even 18-inch wheels/tires is that they have shorter sidewalls for decreased body roll. Tires with stiffer sidewalls are generally easier to break loose and keep spinning. It is also advisable to choose tires that are hard enough to break loose on command, but sticky enough to maintain control and regain traction as you exit a drift. They should also last a little longer and are slightly cheaper than the stickier tires.

FRONT SUSPENSION AND BRAKES

I pulled the fenders off for easy access and pictures; you can bypass this step. Everything about the suspension on this car was old and worn out, but it was nothing I couldn't fix. I started by removing the brakes, struts, knuckles, spindles, the lower transverse links (control arms), and tension rods, as well as the inner and outer tie-rod ends. With everything out of the way, I cleaned up the crossmember and inner fender well with degreaser and touched it up with a little flat black spray paint.

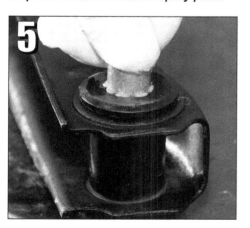

Next, the metal sleeve was greased up and slid into place-these too are a really tight fit. These bushings were relatively easy to install, as the rest of the kit requires the bushings be pressed in. Be careful: the grease gets everywhere and is impossible to get off of anything. As long as you have a press, a torch and some patience, you can do this install yourself.

Even if you know what you're doing, removing the knuckle spindle from the ball joint on the transverse link can be tough. You can use a ball joint removal tool (pickle fork), but if you don't have one, you can use a pry bar to put tension on the spindle and then hit the side of the ball joint seat until the two come apart. You never want to hit the threaded ball joint shaft.

Once you have everything cleaned up and ready to go, it's time to start installing the new parts. Here, a new outer tie-rod end from Napa is being threaded onto the beefy inner tie-rod end from JIC Magic. The inner tie-rod end simply threads onto the steering rack and is covered by a rubber boot.

To install the Energy Suspension polyurethane bushings into the transverse link, I first had to press out the factory bushing (it can also be removed with heat) and then lubricate the metal shell before pushing in the two Energy Suspension bushing halves. These bushings are designed to be precise and reduce unwanted movement, so they are a really tight fit.

Even the tension rods receive a set of three-piece Energy Suspension bushings. I started by lubricating everything then pushed the bushings into place and inserted the metal sleeve. These rods come with a large rubber bushing from the factory so that they'll move backwards a little when you hit a bump. This makes for a smooth factory ride, but for drifting, the more precise handling and extra road feel of the stiffer polyurethane is preferable.

I also decided to install a new ball joint before I reinstalled the transverse link. I found these hefty Napa ball joints were much beefier than the factory units and came complete with a zerk fitting so that they could be greased regularly, unlike the stock units. I Just press out the old ball joints and press in the new ones. It's pretty tricky to balance that odd-shaped control arm on the press, but it's possible.

The tension rod just slid into place in the bracket and bolted up to the transverse link. All of the bushing surfaces that came in contact with metal were greased prior to installation.

Once the ball joint was properly seated in the transverse link, all I had to do was install the C-clip, zerk fitting (it was turned inward toward the transverse link so I would have access to it even with the wheel in place), and the rubber boot that came with it.

A freshly painted knuckle spindle, minus the brake baffle plate, was dropped into place on the ball joint. The large sealed bearing in the spindle on my car showed no signs of play so I left it in place. To remove the baffle plate I had to unbolt the hub from knuckle spindle, remove it, pull the baffle plate off, and then put the assembly back together. You have to remove or trim the baffle plate on any car with upsized rotors.

With all its new parts installed, the transverse link simply bolted back into place on the 240's front suspension member. Of course, everything was cleaned and painted prior to installation. Notice the inner and outer tie-rod ends and the boot that were installed earlier.

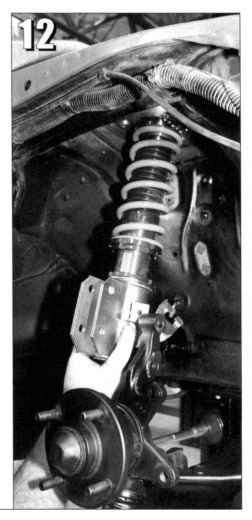

I slipped the JIC Magic coil-over into place and secured it on top with one of the three nuts that will eventually hold it and a strut tower brace in place. The other end was bolted to the knuckle spindle with the factory nuts and bolts. As you can see, installing coil-overs really isn't that difficult. And since many different drift cars start with a MacPherson front suspension, your coil-over install should be very similar.

After I lowered the car back down, I installed the front DC Sports strut tower bar onto the coil-over studs and then tightened down the factory bolts. Besides exceptional production quality, you will notice that this strut bar doesn't have any moving parts that would allow it to flex or shift.

With all the suspension in place, I was able to install the new brakes. I set the rotors in place on the studs and then installed brake pads into the new calipers before bolting them to the knuckle spindle with the factory bolts. Various other big brake upgrade kits will come with all the necessary hardware and brackets for your particular vehicle, but otherwise should go on just as easily as these did.

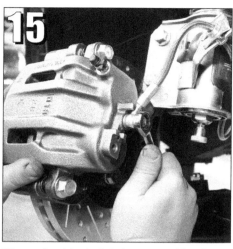

These braided stainless steel brake lines bolt to the caliper with the factory banjo bolt and fresh copper crush washers. After that, I installed the mounting clip to hold the line in place. The far end of the line bolted up to the car's hard line. Tighten it down with a flare nut wrench to avoid rounding the nut.

These Progress Group sway bars simply bolt in place of the factory units with the provided polyurethane bushings, brackets, and hardware (the Energy Suspension bushings won't work because they were designed for the smaller-diameter stock bar). After the bushings were installed to secure the bar, end links were installed between it and the lower control arms.

I chose the outermost mounting hole on the Progress bar, which is the softest setting. This should help keep traction at the front wheels and reduce understeer. Of course this is just a starting point, and I will adjust both the front and rear sway bars as needed once I put in some track time.

The completed front suspension not only looks great, but provides me with a number of benefits that will aid in my drifting efforts.

REAR SUSPENSION AND BRAKES

Now it's time to move on to the rear suspension and brakes. Everything I'm going to reuse is intact and in decent shape. All the parts that were worn or damaged will be replaced or upgraded.

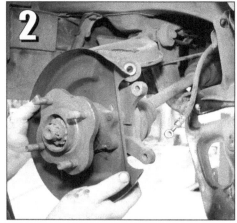

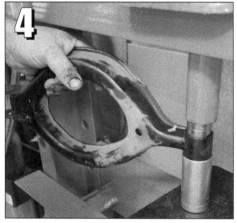

Up front, there were only six rubber bushings to replace with polyurethane; there are three times that many in the rear. The 240's adjustable independent rear suspension is one of the reasons this car is so popular for drifting, but it does make for a lot more work when you're changing out all the bushings! For this reason, I decided to remove the entire suspension including the half shafts and knuckle spindle.

Besides all the front and rear bushings, the Energy Suspension Set even includes rear subframe inserts. These inserts fit into a gap built into the existing subframe bushings. They help to further stiffen the 240's chassis by reducing unwanted flex and movement between the subframe and unibody. To install them, I removed one subframe bolt at a time and slid an insert into place. After that, a large washer was installed over the factory bolt to hold the insert in place.

Many of your factory rubber bushings will need to be pressed out or removed with heat. I chose to press out as many as possible because it doesn't make as much of a mess. To put it mildly, the factory bushings don't want to come out, so upgrading them is a time-consuming job. Be careful not to damage the piece you are removing the bushing from (such as this upper control arm), as you may need to apply so much pressure that you bend the steel.

After you remove the factory bushings, apply a liberal amount of grease and then press the new bushing into place. This is trickier than it sounds because even though the bushings are rigid, they can fold up under the pressure of the press. Basically, I had to make sure each bushing was perfectly centered over the piece it was being pressed into and that the edges folded up evenly all the way around as it slid into place. After each bushing is in place, grease and press in a steel sleeve.

You can also remove a bushing by torching it out. This is a messy job that I would rather have passed on, but not all bushings can be pressed out. Be careful not to damage any of the parts—and don't set anything on fire! Basically, you just heat the metal surrounding the bushing until the rubber melts and the bushing falls out. You'll probably still have to clean the excess rubber out of the inner diameter of each location.

In some cases, as with the lower control arm, not only do you have to remove the bushing, but the pressed-in bushing shell as well. You can't press out the shell, but you can cut through it with a hacksaw to release its preload.

Releasing the preload is only half the battle. Use a brass punch to hammer out the unwanted shell. This is fairly difficult because there is almost no edge on which to place the punch. Once you get it going, the sleeve should slide right out.

There are some polyurethane bushings you need to install where you can't use the press. This is where a vice can come in handy. It's tough to get the first edge in evenly, but once you do, the bushings should slip easily into place. The new steel sleeves can be pressed in the same way.

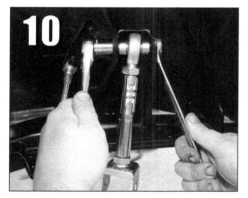

With all the bushings installed, it was time to start bolting parts back onto the car. I started with these JIC-Magic fully adjustable Rear Toe Control Arms. They simply bolt in place of the non-adjustable factory piece. These control arms use solid, spherical bearings in place of sloppy rubber bushing. I will now be able to adjust the rear wheel toe, either in or out, which will have an effect on both traction and tire wear.

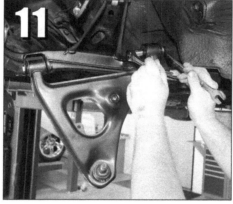

The lower control arm, lower rear link, and upper rear link are bolted to the car using the factory hardware. The upper and lower links are mounted on offset cam bolts that allow for adjustment of caster and camber. Once the car was on the ground, I took it to Network Alignment in Phoenix for a four-wheel alignment. The idea was to achieve a good baseline alignment, and then make minor adjustments from there at the track.

Once all the link bars and the lower control arms were in place I installed the rear JIC Magic coil-overs. Just as in front, the coil-over simply slid into place and was secured with the factory nuts after the rear DC Sports strut tower bar was set in place. This may seem like an odd order for installation, but because I had to install the relatively heavy rear axle and hub assembly, complete with the halfshaft, I wanted to bolt them up to the coil-overs, which would hold them in place.

I set the complete axle hub assembly into place and secured it to the coil-over. Then the front and rear upper link bars, lower link bars, and control arms were all bolted to the axle housing.

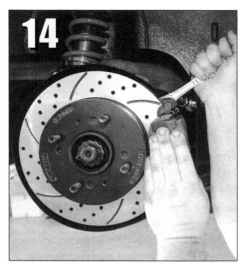

After all the various rear suspension parts were installed, it was time for the brakes. The new rotors just slid into place—note that they actually fit inside the baffle plate. I cleaned up the factory 240 caliper and installed new brake pads before I bolted it in place over the rotor.

Once the sway bar install was complete, I reinstalled the last section of the Bullet exhaust system. Know that the settings I recommended for the front and rear sway bars are just good starting points, as are all of the initial suspension settings that I have suggested in this chapter. Ideally, knowledge of each component, along with sufficient track time, will help you learn how their setup affects your drifting. That is the best way to determine how you should tune your various suspension components.

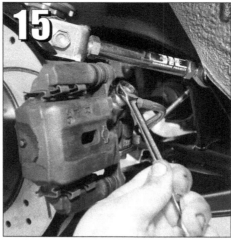

The worn rear factory rubber brake lines were replaced with braided stainless steel lines. I secured one end of the line to the caliper with the factory banjo bolt and fresh crush washers, and attached the other end to the factory hard line.

The new rear suspension has all the adjustability of the front and more.

I installed an adjustable Progress Group sway bar out back. I wanted the rear suspension to be stiffer and have less body roll to help make breaking the rear tires loose more predictable and consistent. I will be able to use the sway bar, along with the other tunable rear suspension components, to dial in more or less traction at the rear tires. Although you want to reduce traction at the rear wheels of a drift car to initiate a drift, you still need some traction to maintain a drift.

With the suspension finished off I installed on these Konig Hurry Wheels and Falken Azenis tires. I chose these relatively lightweight 17-inch wheels not only because they were affordable, but because I like how they look, too—I figure if I'm going to be out drifting, I might as well look good doing it. I'm also installing a set of Falken tires on the stock steel wheels that came with the car just to be sure I have tires with enough tread to drive home on after a day at the track. Even if you trailer your car to an event, you will still want a set of spare wheels and tires so you can be sure to get in a full day of drifting, even if you wear out your first set of tires.

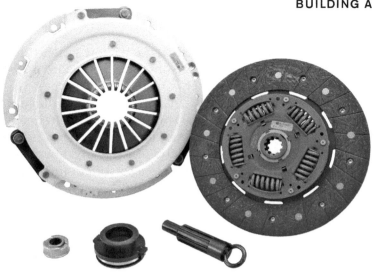

If your stock clutch works, use it while you can. Once it begins to slip, swap it out for a superior high-performance setup—replacing it with a stock clutch will only be a waste of time and money. An aftermarket performance clutch and pressure plate will not only last longer then stock, but will offer increased torque capacity and clamp load—two very important elements to consider when utilizing the Clutch Kick, Shift Lock, and various other drift initiation techniques. This particular clutch kit from ACT is for the late-model Mustang, but with over 300 applications, you can probably find one for your car. (Advanced Clutch Technology ACT)

Drivetrain Upgrades

The differential is the first thing to consider when assessing and upgrading your drift car's drivetrain. Most cars come from the factory with an open differential, which will allow one of the drive wheels to be stopped completely while the other one receives all of the power. An open differential is used by auto manufacturers to make their cars comfortable and

safe to drive, by the average person, in a variety of conditions. Specifically, when you drive a car in a circle, the outside drive wheel travels farther than the inside one; an open differential allows the drive wheels to do this.

An LSD, or limited-slip differential, minimizes the drive wheels' ability to move independently and sends power to both equally, depending on percent of lock, which makes it much easier to

break both rear tires loose. The LSD is not as user-friendly on the street for this very reason— but this shouldn't be an issue for your drift car. Lock refers to how much or how little the drive wheels can move independently of each other. For example an LSD with 100% lock will not allow the drive wheels much leeway at all, whereas 70% lock will allow one wheel slightly more movement independent of the other—but nowhere near as much as an open differential.

Of course, you can start out with an open differential, and there are those out there who say you should. On the other hand, the inconsistency of an open differential, where one wheel could break traction while the other may or may not, can make learning slightly more difficult. For this reason I suggest anyone into drifting should upgrade to an LSD as soon as possible. Only your experience with drifting and budget can really

This is the much-coveted KAAZ LSD. In drifting, an LSD will make life much easier when you are trying to break both rear wheels loose to initiate a drift. With an open differential one wheel could break traction while the other may or may not.

determine when you should make the upgrade.

If your specific car didn't come with an LSD from the factory, you may be able to swap one in from a higher-performance version of the same car, or you could source one from the aftermarket. If you do buy a car with an LSD, either factory or aftermarket, you should probably remove it and rebuild it to make sure it's up to factory specifications or better. Various companies sell kits with all the necessary hardware for this service, including friction discs. You want to make sure your differential is tight and strong as you will be putting a lot of stress on it as you both initiate and maintain a drift.

You will upgrade the clutch in your drift car—whether you first intend to or not. It's easy to dismiss the clutch as it is out of sitght and out of mind. However, if you're drifting, it won't forget you. You have to think about the clutch in your drift car just like one of the tires. It is a wear item that you use constantly when drifting. Your clutch is put under extremely harsh conditions, so it is crucial that you upgrade it. You can get a few practice runs out of the stock clutch that comes with your drift car if it is in good working order, so you may as well get some use out of it. If it slips right from the start however, change it out immediately.

There really is little reason to swap out one stock clutch for

another. Because of how much time it takes to install a new clutch, it's definitely worth the money to upgrade to a stronger, more durable unit. You will still wear out aftermarket clutches, just not as fast as stock units. On top of longevity, aftermarket clutches also offer increased clamping pressure.

Know that when I say "clutch," I'm referring to the clutch disc, pressure plate, and even the flywheel. You won't have to replace your flywheel as often, but it will get scored and have to be re-surfaced a few times before it will need to be replaced. The pilot and throwout bearings should also be replaced whenever you install a new clutch and pressure plate.

LSD INSTALL

Believe it or not, installing an LSD is relatively easy. Remove the exhaust section from under the differential carrier housing. Support the carrier housing with a floor jack. Unbolt the driveshaft and both halfshafts from the housing, and then unbolt the housing from the rear suspension member. Carefully lower the housing out of the car. Rotating the housing slightly will help it clear the sway bar and halfshafts.

I had Doug's Performance Transmission in Mesa, Arizona, help me with the shims and check the gear lash. Once at Doug's, Michael Jackson (no, seriously) made quick work of tearing my differential apart. It was pretty dirty, but all the parts I needed were in good shape. Check out the open differential just to the left of the housing. The KAAZ LSD is much stronger than the stock diff. After a quick dip in the hot tank, everything needed to complete the job was laid out in the clean room for assembly.

Start by installing the ring gear onto the LSD. It's a tight fit, so just slide it in as far as you can, and then pull it in the rest of the way with the bolts. Make several passes around the differential, tightening each bolt to spec little by little, to make sure the ring gear doesn't bind up.

With the ring gear in place, slip the new bearings and races in place on either side of the differential. Install the differential into the carrier housing using three spacers. Notice that in our install, one of the spacers on this side didn't quite make it.

With some gentle motivation, that third spacer fell into line and everything fit together perfectly. If your factory shims don't fit, you can always buy a kit with various shims and install the proper thickness on each side of the differential. In hindsight, knowing that the KAAZ LSD fit well enough to use the factory shims, I probably could have done the job myself, and so can you.

Once everything is in place, install the end caps and secure them with the factory bolts. Though I didn't show it in the pics, it's important that you use a torque wrench to snug things up to the factory specs. After the LSD is secured, check the ring and pinion gears for lash.

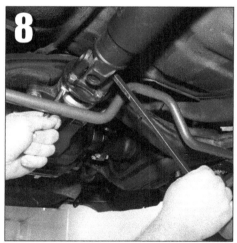

Use a mallet to gently tap the new rubber seals into place. Then slide the side flanges into place and seat them with the palm of your hand. Finally, install a new seal and the differential cover. Once that was complete, the differential was filled with KAAZ 80W90 gear oil. You can actually use this gear oil in both your LSD and manual transmission. KAAZ claims its gear oil will increase LSD life while reducing noise.

To install the differential carrier housing with the new LSD installed, I put it back on the floor jack and lifted it into place. Installation is the reverse of the removal. Bolt the half shafts to the side flanges and reinstall the driveshaft. The bolts don't spin on the driveshaft side thanks to a stop, but I used a breaker bar to keep the driveshaft from turning while I tightened the nuts on the other side.

The completed LSD did set me back about $900, but the first time I drove the car I knew it was worth every penny. Besides making it easier to break both rear tires loose at the same time, the new LSD is much more durable than the stock unit. This is a good thing considering how much stress the differential experiences when you initiate, maintain, and even exit a drift.

Engine Upgrades

Should you upgrade the engine in your drift car? That depends on the car, its weight, and its stock power level. For the most part, every drift car out there has, at the very least, some bolt-on performance-enhancing devices-cold-air intake, exhaust, downpipe, engine management, etc. Many times, stock engines are swapped out altogether for more powerful units. And then there's forced induction. Whether it's a supercharger or an upsized turbo, forced induction is extremely popular in drifting.

To start off, yes, you can drift with a stock engine. As long as it can break the rear tires loose on command, your stock engine is fine. And, as I have said several times throughout this book, it's a good idea to start out with a stock car. I would also recommend putting money into your suspension before you increase your car's horsepower.

Up from stock, you can add bolt-on equipment that will free up a few extra horsepower without breaking the bank. Don't just throw on an intake and exhaust because everyone else does. Instead, do your homework and only purchase the parts that will add the power you want. How much power each

part adds will depend on the part itself, your car, and the other mods you've done.

Ultimately you have to ask yourself, "Will the part(s) I am adding make it easier for me to drift?" For example, an intake and exhaust may only give you around 10 hp, and you may not even be able to feel that. However, installing and intake, exhaust, turbo outlet, and downpipe (assuming this is a turbocharged car), along with a tunable engine management system, may offer you a much more significant gain. Of course, all this will cost a lot more money, which is one more reason to do your homework before you buy.

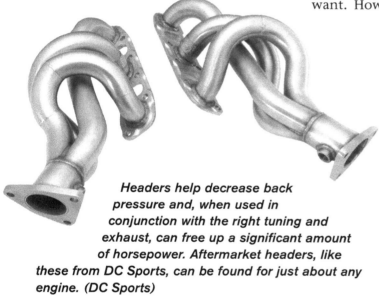

Headers help decrease back pressure and, when used in conjunction with the right tuning and exhaust, can free up a significant amount of horsepower. Aftermarket headers, like these from DC Sports, can be found for just about any engine. (DC Sports)

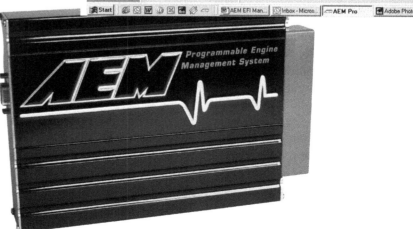

It doesn't matter how big your engine is, or how many performance parts you bolt on-if your engine isn't tuned properly, it won't provide maximum performance. Aftermarket engine management systems like this unit from AEM give virtually limitless control over your engine. (Advanced Engine Management, AEM)

A free flowing exhaust system is a simple and relatively inexpensive way to free up a few extra horsepower. Various manufacturers offer bolt-in systems that you can install yourself, or you can have a custom exhaust system fabricated at a local muffler shop. Plus they sound cool, too. (DC Sports)

Intakes like this AEM Brute Force unit not only allow more air to flow freely into your engine than a stock air box, but when properly designed, will draw in the coolest air available. In some cases, this means positioning the large air filter outside the engine bay or moving it as far away from heat sources as possible and incorporating a heat shield. (Advanced Engine Management, AEM)

Regardless of what parts you do buy, make sure they will work with future upgrades. You don't want to spend money on a part that will need to be swapped out when you make other upgrades down the line.

Engine swaps are hugely popular in the tuner market. Many of the imported drift cars boast a larger, more powerful engine transplanted from another car. This is because engine swaps are a good, reliable way to increase your horsepower while still retaining a stock, or relatively stock, engine. Of course, engine swaps can be time consuming and expensive. And, it can be very difficult to troubleshoot problems or find parts on a car that has an engine other than stock. If you do choose to increase horsepower by way of an engine swap, make sure there is available information on how to do the swap, and how to troubleshoot problems. You also need to make sure you can get both stock and aftermarket parts for the engine you want to install.

Even if you swap in a turbocharged engine, one of the more popular upgrades is a larger turbo. For the most part, the engines themselves are left stock internally as they were originally built to handle more power than they actually put out. So upsizing the turbo and opening up the exhaust, as well as tuning this new system with the appropriate engine management, can be a great way to increase horsepower. But all of this doesn't come cheap, and that is why such extensive modifications are typically only found on professional drift cars. And of course, the more horsepower you make with a stock engine, the better chance something will break.

Engine swaps and turbos may be popular with the imports, but domestic muscle is all about the supercharger. In many cases a supercharger and a free-flowing exhaust, tuned with the proper engine management, is all the extra motivation a V-8 needs. Of course, many domestic V-8s come with plenty of low-end torque from the factory.

Regardless of how you increase the power in your drift car, you want to make sure it is reliable power. You don't want to try squeezing 400 hp out of an engine that's only able to comfortably produce 300. If you tune an engine to the breaking point on the dyno, it will certainly fail under the harsh conditions of drifting. This is why it's better to swap in a more powerful stock engine than build-up a less powerful one, as you will probably be sacrificing reliability.

Cooling may actually be more important than horsepower. The cooling system in every car on the road today was designed to do its job when the car is traveling in a straight line. When drifting, your car will be traveling at a given angle, which means the cooling system will not be working at its optimum level. On top of that, you'll be pushing your drift car extremely hard. These two factors make drift cars run extremely hot, be sure the cooling system is up to the task.

Install a larger, aluminum, multi-core radiator and make sure you flush the system regularly. You can also install an electric fan in place of the clutch fan, but be sure it comes with a shroud that helps it pull air through the whole radiator. An electric fan frees up an extra horsepower or two and can be set to maximum at all times, even after the engine is turned off. They say the clutch fan spins relative to engine RPM, so it doesn't cool as much when the car is at low RPM.

Interior Upgrades

One way to increase performance without adding horsepower is to decrease weight—and you can gut the interior of your drift car for free. You don't need various interior panels, rear seats, a stereo, or sound deadening. Besides increasing your power-to-weight ratio, gutting your drift car's interior to this level will also allow valuable feedback from the road through to your ears and the rest of your body.

One of the things you do need in your drift car is a good racing seat, specifically one with large side bolsters to keep your body from moving side to side when you drift. The seat should also be covered in a fabric that doesn't let you slide around like leather or vinyl. This seat will also have little padding and thus will better transmit information from the car through to

your body. It should be positioned at a distance from the steering wheel that requires your arms to be bent at just about 90 degrees when you grip it. Your knees should also be bent slightly when you put them on the pedals so that you have full access to their complete range of travel before you straighten out your legs.

To further keep your body in place, and for added safety, you should install a 5-point racing harness. To do this, you have to first install a roll cage. The reason is that in the event of a roll-over, you would not be able to move your head, so you need the roll cage to protect it. The harness will also bolt to the cage. You wouldn't even be able to pass a vehicle tech inspection at a race or drift event if you had a 5-point harness without the proper roll cage. On top of safety, a roll cage will further stiffen up your chassis.

You may not think a steering wheel is that big of a deal, but this is the control you will use the most in drifting, so it needs to be comfortable and conducive to the task at hand. The steering wheel in your drift car should be completely round and the same thickness all the way around. This is because you will use every inch of the steering wheel hoop as you turn in, countersteer and unwind the steering wheel from one corner to the next. Notice the yellow band at the top of this SPW wheel. It will allow you a visual reference of how far the wheel is turned.

Your shift knob and pedals should be easy to access from the driver's seat and should not distract your attention from driving at any time. You don't want a loose shift knob or large, slippery aftermarket pedal covers that will get in your way when you are trying to focus on the task of drifting.

When looking for a steering wheel, everything I found was either really expensive or cheap and not designed for drifting. Then I stumbled upon the SPW Type 4, which features a continuous round hoop with three small spokes that are less likely to get in the way as you steer. It even has a yellow band at the top for quick visual reference of how far it is turned—this is a great tool for beginners and advanced drifters alike. This steering wheel will fit on any car with the right hub adapter, and you can get both for around $120.

Drifting is precision driving, and it's no time to be playing around with a sloppy shifter. This precision short-throw shifter from B&M has a very solid feel and short throw so that you can shift quickly and accurately up and down through the gears. Best of all, B&M has a model that will bolt directly into the SR20DET transmission goes for under $200.

106   HOW TO DRIFT: THE ART OF OVERSTEER

Installing a roll cage in your drift car is a great idea. Not only will it make your car safer, and allow you to safely run a set of 4- or 5-point harnesses, it also will make your chassis more rigid. If you plan on drifting competitively, you'll need to install a serious multi-point roll cage that conforms to the sanctioning body's rule book. Basic bolt-in roll cages are just for show and don't count. (Travis Thompson)

The factory 240 seats aren't that bad, as they have fairly large side bolsters for stock seats. The seats in my car were pretty well worn and the upholstery was torn and loose in a few spots. Luckily, I found these new V-Racing seats on clearance for $50 each! To mount them I fabricated a pair of steel brackets so that they would sit as close to the floor as possible and far enough back so that I would be comfortable and have good access to the controls. There aren't any sliders, so basically this car is set up just for me, or someone my height.

SHIFTER INSTALL

When I tried to unbolt the shifter base from the transmission and remove it, the gasket was so old and dried onto both pieces that I couldn't get them to budge. I actually had to use a small pry bar to separate them. After that, the remnants of the old gasket were scraped off the transmission. I waited to install the B&M shifter so that I could install the engine and transmission in the car as a single unit. The shifter opening was taped up before the engine and transmission were installed.

I also smeared some grease on the nylon pivot ball prior to the shifter's installation. I simply lined this piece up with the shifting mechanism in the transmission.

Once the transmission was in the car and ready for the shifter I applied a liberal amount of black RTV silicone to the bottom of the shifter to form a gasket around its outer edge. Loop around each mounting hole to ensure there will be no leaks.

Now comes the hard part, slipping the shifter base through the hole in the transmission tunnel without getting any silicone on anything or scraping it off the bottom of the shifter base. Carefully position the shifter over the opening in the transmission and align the nylon pivot ball with mechanism in the transmission that it snaps into.

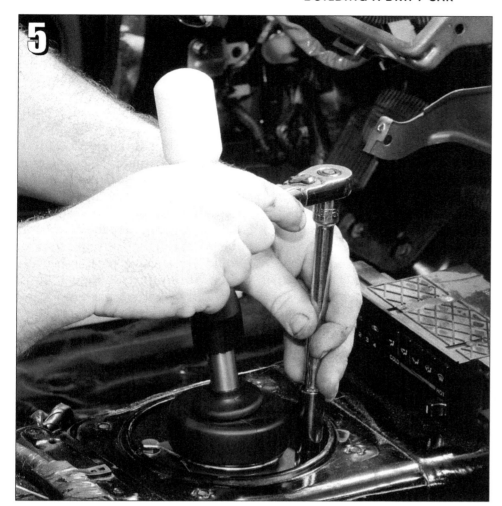

Once everything is lined up, push down firmly to snap the pivot ball into place and then install four of the six 12-mm bolts that you can access through the opening in the transmission tunnel.

Below: Finally, I installed the factory rubber shift boot and secured it with the steel retaining ring and four 10-mm bolts. I also installed a very comfortable leather shift knob from B&M. The center console and a factory vinyl boot that I got on eBay (remember this car originally had an automatic transmission) will be installed later. Upgrading to an aftermarket shifter will ensure smooth, precise shifting, and installation will be very similar for any front engine, RWD car. If you choose to keep your stock shifter, make sure it is free of any slop, and that it has a secure and comfortable shift knob.

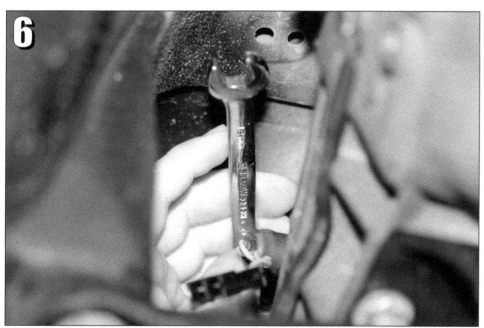

The forward two bolts that hold the B&M shifter in place need to be installed from under the car—luckily I had a lift.

Exterior Upgrades

As for the exterior of your drift car, you don't need anything special. Body kits are just for looks, and in most cases so are wings. A truly functional wing will provide maximum downforce when the car is traveling at speed, in a straight line, assuming the wing is high enough off the deck lid. When you are drifting at maximum slip angle, airflow across a wing is not ideal, but it will provide some downforce. This downforce can provide added traction at the rear tires, so depending on your car and its setup, this could be desirable, but it might not be. Rhys Millen has lateral wings that were inspired by large sprint car wings. They run from his GTO's rear window back to its regular rear wing. These help him maintain a drift at a slip angle greater than he otherwise might be able to—but these are only beneficial to a professional drifter like Rhys. We are starting to see other competitive drivers with large lateral sections on their regular wings that may have been installed with the hope of achieving similar results.

Any modifications to the exterior of a drift car should be to accommodate modifications that aid in drifting. For example, an aftermarket front fascia with large openings that allow air to flow freely over a front-mount intercooler and the car's radiator would be an asset. A carbon fiber hood or fenders that reduce weight would also be a good idea, if your budget allows for them. Other than for useful modifications, however, the exterior of a drift car should be all business. Everything should be securely mounted to the body such as the front fascia, fenders, hood wing, body kit, and side mirrors. Speaking of side mirrors, a pair of mirrors that you can actually see out of would be a good idea, especially when drifting on tandem runs. Drift cars do contact each other and the wall, so a pristine show car isn't the best idea, unless you're okay with getting it dinged up.

You know the purpose of a wing for racing—to provide downforce, which translates to increased traction at the rear wheels. But why would you need one for drifting? Remember that you want reduced rear tire traction in drifting, not the complete lack of traction. In many cases, drivers set up their wing to increase rear tire traction when they aren't getting enough traction to consistently maintain a drift. Notice also that this wing has large side panels, which may have been added so that the air flowing into them will push back on the car and help the driver maintain maximum slip angle without spinning.

FRONT FACIA INSTALL

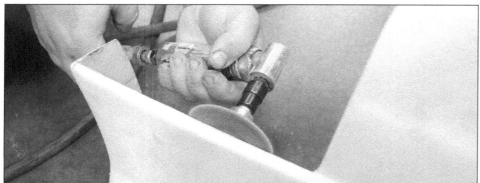

As with any body kit, there was some trimming necessary to make this front fascia fit. It's very difficult for any aftermarket manufacturer to take small automobile variances into account—not to mention that this car certainly isn't as straight as it was when it rolled off the showroom floor. So when the new front fascia was in place I checked all the edges where it met the car and marked any spots that I felt needed trimming. Be careful not to let your right angle grinder (or whatever you use for shaping) grab the fiberglass and take out more material than you want. It only took a few seconds to smooth out this edge and make it flow with the factory fender. I only had to test-fit and trim this piece twice to get it perfect.

I didn't make very many changes to the 240's exterior, with the exception of a carbon fiber hood and this new front fascia from DriftWorks by APC. There are some people who look down on that name, but let me shed some light on these two products. Both the front fascia and carbon fiber hood were easy to come by, they fit just fine with only minor trimming, and they are affordable—not to mention they are lighter than their stock counterparts. Here you can see the fiberglass front fascia (APC calls it an air dam) has much larger openings for better breathing and cooling than the battered stock front fascia that came with my 240.

This is what that edge looked like once the front fascia was set in place. After it was installed for good, I added a couple of screws around the corner in the fender well. You want to make sure everything you install on your drift car is held firmly in place.

The only other things that needed to be trimmed were the holes for the factory marker lights. I used an air saw to cut along the inner edge of the opening, being careful not to cut out the flat spots where I would install speed clips to accept the two screws that hold each light in place.

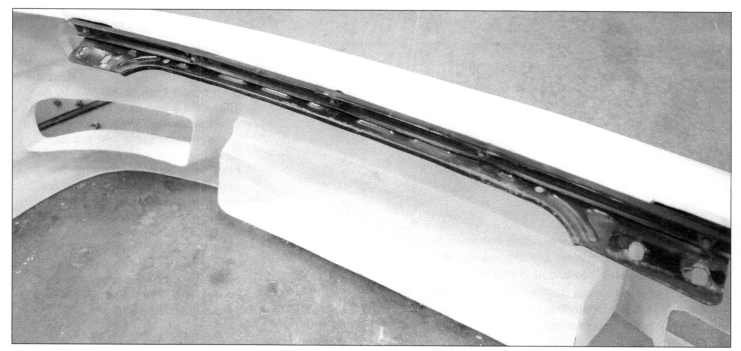

There are several brackets on the factory front fascia, but only this one needs to be removed and installed on the new piece. The DriftWorks front fascia is actually sandwiched between the two pieces of this bracket, which bolts up to the 240's core support.

So why, on a budget, did I choose an aftermarket front fascia for my drift car? Simple: the intercooler. The large openings in the DriftWorks air dam allow cool air to flow freely over the factory side-mount intercooler. And when I'm ready to upgrade to a large front-mount intercooler, there's already an opening in the center that's just right for it. You could use the stock front fascia and just cut hole for the intercooler, but the one that came with my 240 had several cracks and wasn't hanging onto the car by much. Not to mention I liked the look of the DriftWorks piece.

I also installed this carbon fiber hood from DriftWorks. It just bolted in place of the factory hood without any modifications, except for a pair of hood pins to keep it secure. No carbon fiber hood is as rigid as a steel hood, and the three factory mounting points (hood hinges and latch) just aren't sufficient. I found some APC hood pins at my local auto parts store and they help keep it down.

240SX Drift Car Budget

So now you know that this, along with the engine swap covered in the next chapter, is how I spent my $10K budget to build the ultimate entry-level drift car. I have listed all of the big parts I purchased in the chart below and if you read ahead, then you know I spent a whopping $11,419. Yes, I went over budget. Now I could have simply upped the budget to $12K once I was done with the car and you would have been none the wiser. But I set out to build a $10K drift car and I went over budget—it happens. I built this car myself, with my own two hands (and a little help from my friends), and along the way I did my best to make this a real-world example of what it takes to turn a junker into a drifter.

Going over budget is a real possibility, so keep track of what you spend and prioritize your purchases. The bottom line is that I was able to afford going over budget by around 15%, but you have to set a budget you can afford and stick to it as much as you need to. If you can't go over budget, don't. If you come up with a few extra bucks that you don't need to put toward the rent, spend it.

Having built and driven this car, I would prioritize what I did in this order: suspension, tires, LSD, brakes, interior, engine swap, and body mods. Certainly, I could have done without the carbon fiber hood or the front fas-cia in a pinch, and I could have kept the stock seats. If I was on a really tight budget though, I would have found a 240 with a solid KA24DE and saved both time and money on the engine swap. I saved a lot by doing everything, including the engine swap, myself, which is a good thing because there were other expenses along the way. I had to buy silicone, oil, grease, miscellaneous hardware, and more cans of brake cleaner than I want to count. Although these things didn't cost much individually, they still cost money and I suspect all the "little extras" ultimately increased the bottom line of this project by at least another couple of hundred dollars. But hey, I had fun along the way and didn't go completely broke, so I will call this project a success!

What I listed are the big-ticket items and the necessities. Depending on the car you buy, you won't necessarily need everything on this list. The prices are a combination of retail, street prices, sales, and deals-be smart, shop around. I don't buy anything until I Google it or look it up on eBay for reference. I also don't always buy the lowest price I find-you have to weigh out all your options along the way and be a smart consumer. Keep your budget in mind when you set out to build your drift car, and good luck!

This is finished project 240SX. It went slightly over budget, but it was worth it. Most of the advice, budget, and install info applies to other drift cars as well.

Part	Manufacturer	Price
Car		
1992 240SX S13	Nissan	$425
Body		
Carbon Fiber Hood	DriftWorks by APC	$665
Front Fascia	DriftWorks by APC	$350
Hood Pins	APC	$15
Suspension		
FLT-A2 Coilovers	JIC Magic	$1,630
Rear Toe Control Arms	JIC Magic	$279
Inner Tie Rod Ends	JIC Magic	$175
Outer Tie Rod End & Boots	Napa	$89
Anti-roll bars F&R	The Progress Group	$430
Strut Bar	DC Sport (F&R)	$330
Bushings	Energy Suspension	$140
Front Lower Ball Joints	Napa	$75
Brakes		
Front and rear upgrade	Fast Brakes	$700
Wheel and Tires		
Hurry 17 x 7.5	Konig	$425
Azenis 215/40R17	Falken	$368
Engine		
SR20DET Front Clip	Autolink	$2,500
Motor Mounts	NISMO	$200
Filter	K&N	$40
Exhaust Manifold	DC Sports	$359
Exhaust	Bullet by JIC Magic	$383
Transmission		
Clutch	ACT	$370
Clutch hard line	Nissan/Junkyard	$20
Shifter	B&M	$185
Rear End		
Limited-Slip Differential	KAAZ	$895
Interior		
Race Seats (Pair)	V-Racing by Konig	$250
Steering Wheel/Hub Adapter	SPW	$120
	Total	$11,418

SR20DET ENGINE SWAP

I would be remiss to talk about building a 240SX without at least mentioning the legendary 2.0L, dual overhead cam, electronically fuel injected, turbocharged SR20DET powerplant. Available in the S13, S14, and S15 in Japan and other markets (with the exception of the U.S.), Nissan's SR20DET comes in two main flavors—red top and black top. I opted for the more popular and slightly more affordable red top as a transplant for my dear, departed KA24DE.

Before I allow the KA to R.I.P, I feel the need to say a few words on its behalf. There are strong opinions for and against this 2.4L truck motor, but it's a solid choice for drifting. With its relatively large displacement and subsequent torque output, the KA will get the job done. There are also plenty of performance parts available for it, including complete turbo kits. I also found out the hard way that one added benefit to keeping your KA is the availability of stock parts and information. So before you order your SR20DET, do some research on the venerable KA—it might be the right engine for you.

Having said that, the first thing I did after purchasing my 240 was blow a substantial portion of my budget on a complete Silvia SR20DET red top front clip. There are two schools of thought when doing this swap: 1) just buy the engine, transmission, ECU, and harness to save money; 2) buy the whole front clip for parts, reference, and convenience. Because I needed the transmission and wanted to use most of the stock parts that may or may not come with just an engine, I opted for the later. For me, buying the entire front clip turned out to be well worth the extra money, as it not only provided me with the miscellaneous parts that I needed, but it also gave me an idea of where various parts came off the Silvia and where they would wind up on the 240.

Regardless of what you decide to buy, you still need to choose an importer to buy it from. This is not as easy as it sounds, because you can find a red top anywhere from your local newspaper to eBay, but sadly, you can't trust everyone. Rather than search the Internet for a place based solely on appearance and take my chances, I asked around until I found a friend who had a friend who eventually led me to Autolink Motorworks in Temple City, California (www.autolinkmotorworks.com). There I was able to purchase a Sylvia front clip with an SR20DET red top, 5-speed transmission, ECU, uncut harness, intercooler, and bunch of other parts I would need to complete the swap. Because I was referred to Autolink by a friend who had done business with them, I was confident that I would be getting what I paid for and a dependable warranty should something go wrong. Take your time when searching for a front clip. Do some research and ask a bunch of questions up front—it will pay off down the line.

Just as you must beware of shady engine importers, so must you be leery of the engine swap information found on the Internet. There is a lot of information out there, but much of it is incomplete, incorrect, or simply difficult to understand. The most popular site for swap info has to be Heavy Throttle Performance (www.srswap.com). The people there have done a great job of posting much of the information you'll need to install an SR20DET into a U.S. spec 240. Of course, even they don't list all of the little problems that can arise when performing this swap. Still, they are a great resource not only for the swap info, but for engines, parts, and even complete front clips.

I worked my way through all of the engine swap pitfalls so you don't have to. What follows is a real-world example of what it takes for a first-timer to install an SR20DET into a 240SX. Use this information along with your own research to plan for the unexpected. The more you know ahead of time, the easier and faster the swap will go.

PREPPING THE FRONT CLIP

If you've ever wondered exactly what a front clip looks like—well this is it. What you get may vary, as some front clips come complete with a hood, fenders, and headlights although none of this is guaranteed to either be intact or in good condition. You need to make sure you're getting a running engine with good compression over all four cylinders, an ECU, igniter, uncut engine harness, a good 5-speed transmission, and a driveshaft. Everything under the hood should also be intact and in good working condition, as should the factory intercooler, which is located forward of the driver-side front wheel.

If you're swapping an SR20DET into an automatic car, you need the Japanese driveshaft complete with carrier bearing because the U.S. 240 automatic driveshaft is too long. You'll also need the clutch pedal, plus its master and slave cylinders as well. I also made sure my front clip came with a gauge cluster as the Japanese unit reads in kilometers so the U.S. cluster would not be accurate—of course you can always change the sending unit at the transmission to make it work.

The bad part about getting the whole front clip is that you have to pull the engine and that requires removing all the surrounding parts. Start by draining all the fluids, removing the intercooler piping and air filter box, and then take out the radiator and fan shroud. After that, disconnect the power steering and remove all of the wiring from the entire front clip. Unbolt the two engine mounts and the one transmission mount. Before I started, I took dozens of detailed pictures of the engine and front clip for reference.

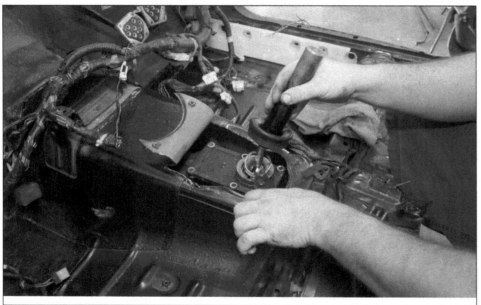

This is about where the upper and lower heater hoses should run once they are mated to their respective heater hoses/adapters in the car (more on that later). Notice that the large bracket is gone but all the grounds have been bolted back in place and an existing bracket was modified to hold the oil feed line. I bent it slightly so I could bolt it to the back of the block in place of the bracket that I removed. The plastic liner in this clip fell apart when I removed it, so I used an extra long piece of rubber hose to run through the bracket. Do all of this and make sure that everything at the back of the block is in perfect working order and leak free, because there is no room to work on anything back there once the engine is in the car.

You'll want to take out the shifter so you can lift the engine and transmission out of the car with an engine hoist. You can either remove the six bolts that secure the base of the shifter to the transmission or remove the internal snap ring that keeps the shifter secured in the base. Because I didn't need the sheetmetal from the front clip, it was no problem to cut away the floor pan for access to the forward two bolts of the shifter base. On my 240, where I didn't want to do this, I accessed these bolts from underneath the car. Once the shifter is out of the way, the two nuts that hold the clutch pedal assembly and master cylinder in place can be removed from the engine bay. Under the dash, take out the Clevis pin that secures the clutch master cylinder's plunger to the clutch pedal and the last bolt that holds the pedal assembly in place. Once I had removed everything from the clip I realized it would be easier to lift the sheetmetal off of the engine/transmission. Depending on your circumstances, you might feel the same way. I unbolted the front crossmember and tilted the sheetmetal up and off of the engine/transmission, and then hoisted it out of the way.

Once the engine is out of the car it can be cleaned up and prepped for installation. The first thing I did was reroute the heater hoses at the back of the engine as they are set up for a right-hand-drive Sylvia and thus running in the wrong direction for the 240. This is what the heater hoses at the back of the engine look like after they come out of the JDM clip. Remove the upper and lower heater hoses and their large bracket.

New engine and transmission mounts are a must. The driver-side mounts in both the front clip and car were completely torn. There are a few options for aftermarket motor mounts, including Cusco and Kazama, but I opted for the Nismo mounts because they are stronger and stiffer than factory and relatively affordable at around $200 for all three pieces. Most other companies sell just the engine mounts for around that much and charge an extra $100 or so for the transmission mount. You can also find the Nismo mounts just about anywhere—I got mine at Intense Motorsports, which is a great source for S13 and other performance parts.

Things get tight once the engine is in its bay, so installing the lower engine harness and oil filter before it goes in the car is a good idea. It's also a good idea to inspect the harness and repair any damage it might have. You can use either your original or the SR20DET harness. I used the SR harness because it had two transmission plugs that the KA harness did not (remember, mine was an automatic). The other end of this harness is connected to the car both at the battery and the fuse box. I had to swap the SR lower harness plug (with the four yellow wires) that makes its connection at the fuse box for the similar plug on the KA lower engine harness. The SR harness had a 6-wire Molex plug, while the KA harness and the plug at the fuse block use a 4-wire Molex plug. This is a simple swap, as the plugs from either harness only have four wires that need to be matched up color to color.

The oil in my new engine was as black as Starbucks French Roast and smelt slightly burnt, but there were no signs of metal shavings or other debris. It is said that in Japan they don't change their oil that often because they only put 30K miles or so on their engines before it becomes too expensive to keep them on the road. Of course this is why low-mileage JDM engines are imported into the U.S. in the first place. Of course, you can use any brand of filter, but your auto parts supplier will look at you funny if you ask for one that fits an SR20DET. Ask for one that fits a '91 Nissan Sentra SE-R with the 2.0L engine. The SE-R happens to run an SR20DE, which is pretty much the same as the SR20DET minus the turbo-many other parts from the SR20DE will work on the SR20DET, but not all of them.

Don't forget the spark plugs. My engine had one NGK plug and three other no-name plugs, all of which needed to be swapped out. I went with Denso Iridium plugs.

A fresh set of belts is also a good idea, so I installed a set of Goodyear Gatorbacks, which are said to be more durable than standard belts. You can get belts specifically for the SR20DET at various sites on the web, or just take yours into an auto parts store and find ones of the same lengths. I just ordered up a set of '91 Sentra SE-R belts. Any auto parts store can cross-reference these belts from one brand to another as well. I used two 4040432 (one for the AC and one for the power steering) and a single 4050370 for the clutch fan/water pump and alternator.

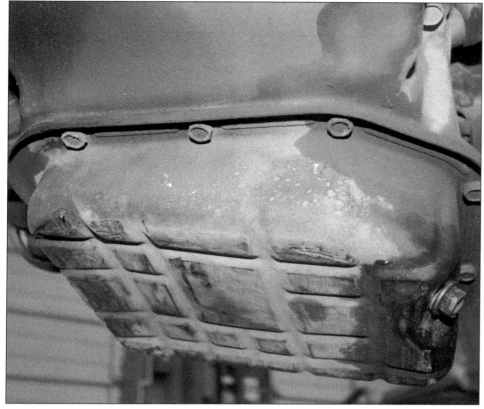

It may be hard to tell, but this oil pan is dented in. The one thing that every site on the web agreed on is that even the smallest dent in your oil pan can cause oil starvation and kill your new engine instantly. I wasn't about to take any chances.

You'll have to remove the oil pan to flatten out any dents. I also inspected and flattened out any of the bolt holes that needed it and cleaned up the pan. With the pan off, it became obvious that the concerns over oil starvation were well founded. Any dent in the pan could keep oil from entering the pickup, which is located very close to the bottom of the pan.

Before I reinstalled the oil pan, I realized I may have actually dented it slightly outward, but that wouldn't be a problem. There is no gasket for this pan, but you can seal it with black RTV silicone. If your budget allows, you can opt for a larger, more durable, cast-aluminum oil pan from GReddy.

CLUTCH INSTALL

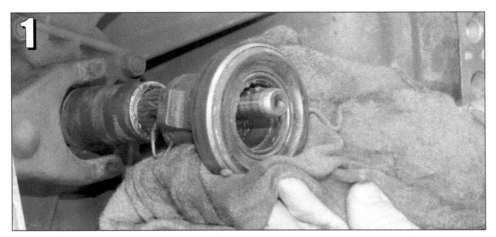

You may be tempted to leave the transmission in place and run with the stock clutch, but doubt led me to pull mine. My clutch disc was worn and my flywheel was heavily scored, which made me realize it would have been stupid to go through all the work and expense of an engine swap only to rely on aclutch that would have been questionable at best. Without a second thought, I ordered an Advanced Clutch Technology (ACT) heavy-duty performance clutch kit. To install a new pressure plate, clutch disc, release bearing, and pilot bearing, I first had to remove the old, worn-out release bearing. It and the release sleeve it is pressed onto can simply be unclipped

Press the release sleeve out from the old throwout bearing and then press the new ACT bearing into place.

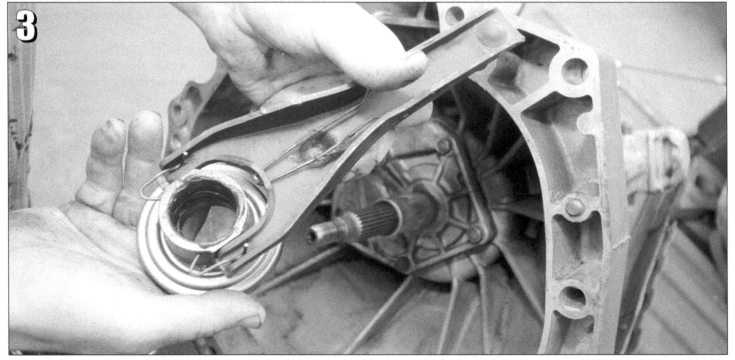

With the new bearing in place, mate the release sleeve to the withdrawal lever with a holder spring. Note that the retainer spring was also in place and lubricated, as was the inside of the release sleeve. You can use a high-quality bearing grease or lithium grease.

Slide the entire assembly into place over the transmission input shaft and snap the retaining spring over the pivot ball. Cover the other end of the release lever, the one that protrudes out of the bell housing, with a dust boot.

The next step is to remove the old and worn pilot bearing from the end of the engine's crankshaft. It took some finesse, but I got mine out. As you can see, it was definitely time for a new one.

Remember to lubricate the new pilot bearing with lithium grease before you gently tap it into place. I used a stubby screwdriver because I knew the plastic handle, which is the only part to come into contact with the bearing, would not damage it. But that only got it so far, so I used a 15-mm socket to gently tap it the rest of the way into place.

Before sandwiching the clutch disc in between the flywheel and pressure plate, I test fit it over the transmission's input shaft. Then the input shaft splines on the transmission were very lightly lubricated. I worked the clutch disc back and forth along the input shaft to distribute the lithium grease evenly over its splines. I also removed any excess grease from the clutch disc's friction surface to keep it from slipping.

The flywheel was pretty badly scored, so I had it resurfaced at Doug's Performance Transmission in Mesa, Arizona, and it looked like new. I cleaned the flywheel with solvent and coated the bolts with Loctite high-temp thread locker before I torqued them to factory specifications. Center the clutch disc over the flywheel with the provided clutch alignment tool and install the pressure plate in place over the disc. I cleaned the pressure plate surface that mates up to the clutch disc prior to installation and coated its bolts with thread locker before I torqued them using a star pattern. Finally, remove the alignment tool and reinstall the transmission back onto the engine. The ACT clutch was well worth the extra effort, as it doubles the factory clamp load, provides increased torque capacity, and will certainly last longer than a stock clutch setup. Street price was around $375.

HEADER INSTALL

That small pipe running up from the turbo outlet is the AIV (air intake valve) pipe. It had to go because the turbo heat shield can interfere with the steering. The DC Sports turbo manifold that was being installed also requires its removal as well as removal of the oil catch can up next to the valve-cover.

While the engine was out, there was one more accessory that I felt the need to install on the new engine—a DC sports stainless steel turbo manifold. Although this is a budget build, and an entry-level drift car that I wanted to keep relatively stock, I felt that it would be a good idea to install this header before the engine was stuffed into the car. This was an upgrade I had already planned for the future, I decided to purchase and install it before the engine was set in place. To install the DC Sports manifold, the oil catch can next to the valvecover had to be removed.

Removing the AIV pipe left us with a large exhaust leak that is best filled with a Plug-Taper (Nissan part number 14052-21R00). You can just cut off the AIV pipe and weld up the threaded fitting that holds it in place, but that takes a certain level of commitment. I wanted to be able put the AIV back if I ever needed to, so I picked up a Plug-Taper from my local Nissan dealer, but you can also get one from Heavy Throttle Performance.

Remove the factory exhaust manifold's heat shield and spray the nuts that hold the manifold to the block with WD-40. Unbolt them along with the four nuts and bolts that secure the manifold to the turbo.

4

The nuts that secure the stock manifold to the turbo are locked into place with steel tabs that simply need to be bent back out of the way. Access to these fasteners is difficult at best. I used a combination of sockets, swivels, extensions, open-end wrenches, and even my fingers to extract them.

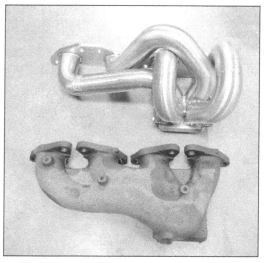

The DC Sports turbo manifold not only looks better than stock, it's also lighter and made up of larger, free-flowing, equal-length runners. This will help exhaust gases flow more freely, build a few extra horsepower, and it should help the turbo spool up faster, which is key when you need to break the tires loose instantly. When you're installing a high-end manifold like this, be careful not to get it too greasy, as any contaminants will leave stains once the engine is started and the manifold gets hot.

5

Once the old manifold was out of the way, I inspected the factory gaskets and determined them to be in good enough shape to reuse. I first set them in place and then installed the DC unit.

The new manifold comes with a mounting bracket, which you set in place on the manifold before you bolt it up. It lines up with all four bolts on the collector and two of the head flange stud holes. Once everything is lined up, the eight factory 10-mm nuts and washers need to be torqued to 43 ft/lbs.

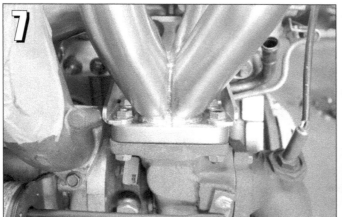

The provided nuts, bolts, and stud that secure the collector to the turbo are a little trickier. The ones closest to the engine only go in from the top down, so the nuts are on the bottom. On the closer side, which you can see here, the forward—most bolt has to be installed from the bottom up with the nut on top. The one stud goes in the hole closest to the master cylinder and gets a nut on the top and bottom—these all get torqued to 16 ft/lbs.

Finally, install the provided 5/8-inch rubber hose between the valvecover and the engine where the oil catch can used to go. I threw on a clamp to make sure it wouldn't move around and come in contact with the manifold. The hose that used to run from the other end of the fitting at the valvecover to the intake was capped with a K&N breather and the hole on the intake was sealed off completely. Once you've finished that, the engine and transmission are ready to be dropped into the 240, but of course there's still a lot more work to be done.

PREPPING THE CAR

It's time to make room for the new engine. My tired and half-torn-apart KA was unceremoniously extracted from the car and set aside. Whatever you do, DON'T get rid of anything until the swap is finished-you never know what you will need until the swap is complete and the car is running.

With the engine out, it's easy to clean the empty engine bay with solvent and a pressure washer. It may not seem like an important step, but it's a good idea to make sure both your engine and engine bay are clean when performing a swap like this so you can easily and quickly trace down leaks. And if you're going through all this trouble, don't you want your drift car to look good?

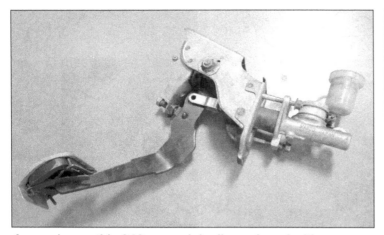

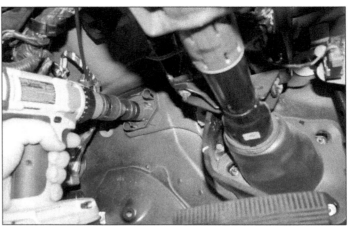

As you know, this 240 was originally equipped with an automatic transmission, which means there was no clutch pedal or clutch master cylinder, but I got these from the front clip. This is just one more reason I opted to buy the entire front clip. Once each of these pieces is positioned on either side of the firewall, those two nuts will hold them together and keep the clutch pedal and clutch master cylinder in place.

Not only did the front clip have almost all the parts I needed to turn this automatic car into 5-speed car—the U.S. 240 also had accommodations for the clutch pedal and master cylinder. Although the holes weren't drilled, this bracket showed exactly where I had to drill the three holes necessary to mount the clutch assembly. The tricky part is making sure the large hole in the middle is properly centered between the mounting stud holes.

Once the holes are drilled, the pedal assembly just drops right in. There is a bolt straight up from the pedal that will hold it in place so that the clutch master cylinder can be installed over the studs that protrude into the engine bay.

The clutch master cylinder just slid right over the mounting studs and was bolted in place with the factory nuts. Inside the car a Clevis pin was installed between the plunger and the clutch pedal arm.

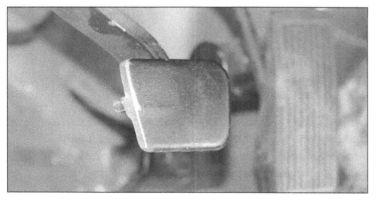

With the clutch pedal in place, it became clear that the extra-wide automatic brake pedal had to go. The easiest way to deal with this is to make a template of the clutch pedal and transfer that shape to the brake. I used a cut-off wheel to eliminate the excess pedal and then trimmed back the gusset behind it so that a factory manual transmission brake pad would fit.

Other than a little adjustment to make the clutch and brake pedals even, installing the third pedal wasn't that bad. Here's the finished product.

To make the clutch system work, I did need to track down one part that I couldn't salvage from the Silvia clip—a left-hand-drive hard line to run from the clutch master cylinder to the slave cylinder. I lucked out and found one in good condition at a Nissan salvage yard just down the street (www.toyotasalvage.com).

The other end of that hard line I picked up from the salvage yard is supposed to be connected to a bleeder valve under the car. You can bypass this if you feel the need, but the one I had looked to be in good condition, so I salvaged it from the clip and it bolted right up to existing holes on the 240. Notice that the slave cylinder was carefully tucked up out of the way prior to installing the engine.

There was one last thing to do before the automatic-to-5-speed swap is complete. This Molex plug is located under the fuse box in the engine bay. These are the automatic transmission starter lockout wires. Install a jumper to connect the heavy-gauge wires (mine were black/yellow and white, but yours may vary) or the car may not start. To access them, you need to remove the two bolts from the side of the fuse box facing the engine and then move the fuse box aside. This Molex plug is attached to the metal mounting bracket that supports the fuse box (I only removed it for the photo). You can install a jumper like this or just cut off the plug and connect the two wires. It might be a good idea to leave the plug in place, just in case.

Then it was time to install the factory side-mount intercooler. It's located on the 240 in the same place it came off of the Silvia clip-just forward of the left front wheel. The 240 had a plastic box in this location that was part of the factory air intake, which I simply unbolted and discarded. From that box, a single pipe ran up through the engine-bay sheetmetal and attached to the factory 240 air intake box, which also needed to be removed. To accommodate the three intercooler pipes and a single vacuum line, I had to make a bigger hole in the sheetmetal. Once again, Nissan made this job a lot easier by having stamped a dimple of the exact shape I needed to cut out, in exactly the right spot. Chris Cowen of Fesler Productions broke out the plasma cutter and made quick work of cutting away the unnecessary sheetmetal. If you don't have access to one, you can open up this area with a hole saw and/or an air saw.

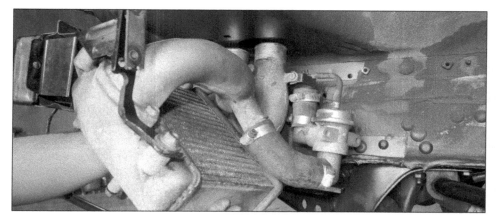

The intercooler itself simply mounts under the car to the same brackets from the plastic air box. Remember to check all the hose clamps to make sure they are snug and provide an airtight seal. I also clocked each of the clamps so that I would have easy access to them once the intercooler was in the car—it would suck to pull it back out just for access to a hose clamp. There's also a single vacuum line that runs up the middle of the three intercooler pipes. Install it before you install the intercooler pipes in the engine bay, as you will not have access to it once they are in place.

Here is what the three pipes from the intercooler look like from inside the engine bay (the small vacuum line fitting is in the center, trust me). Note that the edge of the sheetmetal was covered with a piece of large vacuum line split down one side. Also check out the charcoal canister. It and its mounting bracket came off the front clip and bolted up in place of the 240's charcoal canister bracket. The 240's charcoal canister is bigger and won't fit with the new SR20DET radiator and fan shroud. Why keep it at all? In Arizona, we can pass smog with an engine swap as long as all the emissions equipment is in place and working. Laws about engine swaps and emissions equipment vary drastically from state to state and even city to city, so make sure you do your homework if you plan on doing an engine swap and driving your car on the street.

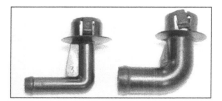

This is a small detail, but there is a plastic fitting on the chassis just below the charcoal canister. The larger one is off the 240, while the smaller one came from the front clip. I needed the smaller one, which snapped into place on the 240 to accept the hose coming out of the bottom of the charcoal canister. I probably could have gotten by without this, but I used it since I had it.

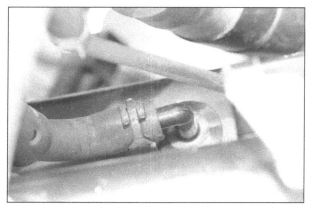

This is how the fitting and the hose from the charcoal canister are positioned, underneath the factory air box.

Besides just attending to engine-specific preparation before the SR was set in place, I also did any work in the engine bay that needed to be done while I had easy access. I greased and installed the Energy Suspension polyurethane bushings for the steering rack. Oddly enough, this car was missing one of the steering-rack brackets, but I got one from the front clip. I did have to remove the heat shield from the bracket that I used, but other than that, the JDM and U.S. brackets are exactly the same.

INSTALLING THE ENGINE

Finally, after a seemingly never-ending amount of work and time, the new engine and transmission were prepped, the 240 was ready to go, and I was finally able to drop the assembly into the car. For this task, you'll need a couple friends and a good engine hoist, to help you out. I have a sturdy Craftsman hoist and after using it, I will never use one of those generic auto parts store hoists again. As you can see, I needed to push down on the transmission so that it would clear the firewall and then lower and move the engine into the car little by little. It's a tight fit to say the least. Once you get the transmission in far enough, put a floor jack under it to level the engine and transmission back out. After all that, it didn't seem like the engine would go far enough back so that the motor mounts would drop into place. It was Chris Cowen who finally worked the mounts into place—thanks Chris!

Bolt down the motor mounts from under the car, securing the engine to the car once and for all. Now you can mount the slave cylinder to the transmission. Fill the clutch master cylinder with high-quality DOT3 brake fluid and bleed the system.

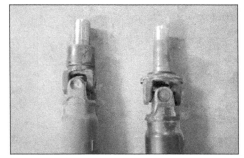

The driveshaft is next in line. Notice the difference between the automatic 240 driveshaft on left and the SR shaft on the right. They are lined up at the other end so you can see that the 240 shaft is longer overall, and the SR shaft has a longer and slightly rustier, spline stub. I used the SR driveshaft on this car. You could also use a U.S. 240SX 5-speed driveshaft with an SR20DET 5-speed transmission, but you have to use the dust collar from the U.S. 240's transmission.

I cleaned the surface rust off the SR driveshaft with some Scotch Bright. Because it came out of the transmission I just installed, the SR shaft fit perfectly into the transmission's slip yoke and the carrier bearing supports lined up perfectly with the bolt holes on the 240. The length was just right as well, and the flanges on the driveshaft and differential lined up perfectly.

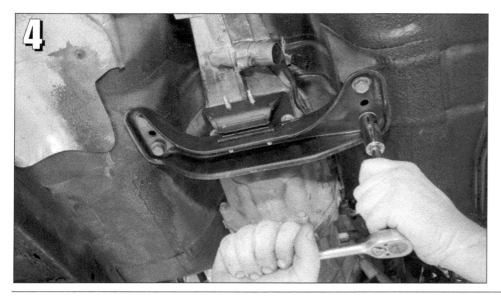

Install the Nismo transmission mount (part number 11320-RS541) and the transmission crossmember when you secure the engine mounts. At this point I was simply making sure they were tight before installing the catalytic converter hanger.

EXHAUST INSTALL

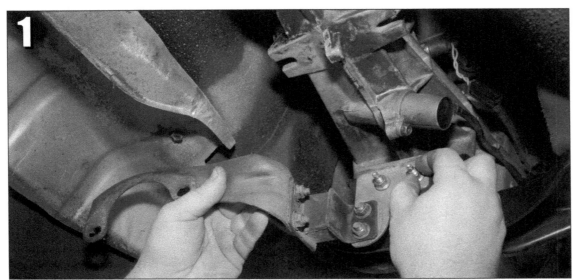

First, install the exhaust bracket from the front clip that holds the downpipe in place under the car. You can tighten it down later, once the catalytic converter and exhaust system are completely installed.

The factory downpipe comes next. Use a fresh gasket and bolt it back up to the factory turbo outlet. I decided to scrap the heat shield, which was barely hanging on, to avoid a few rattles. I know what you're thinking at this point: Why a custom exhaust manifold with a stock turbo and downpipe? Simply put: the budget. An exhaust manifold would have been difficult to swap out down the line, the turbo and downpipe are easier to get to and will take very little time to swap out.

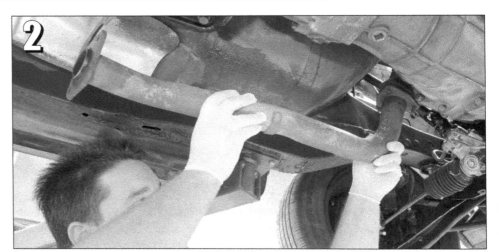

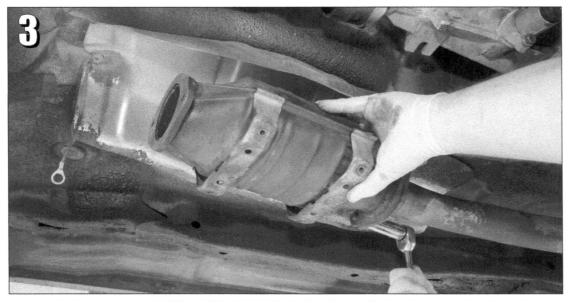

I then bolted the catalytic converter from the front clip in place. The bracket I installed on the transmission mount earlier helps support it by way of the two bolts that secure it to the downpipe. The converter wasn't plugged up, so I decided to retain it in favor of a balanced budget—for the time being. If you have the budget, just replace yours with a high-flowing unit.

Alright, enough of the stock stuff. Yes, I wanted to stay within a budget, and yes I did want to keep my new SR20DET mostly stock. But a few bolt-on performance upgrades along the way to maximize power seems perfectly reasonable. Besides, I needed an exhaust because the one that came on the 240 was trashed. I opted for the $600 S13505SU-FM1 stainless steel Bullet exhaust rather than the Titanium 505TI, which goes for around twice that much. With its incredible all-stainless-steel construction, free-flowing mandrel bent tubing, and straight-through N1-style muffler, the Bullet exhaust was worth the toll it took on my wallet.

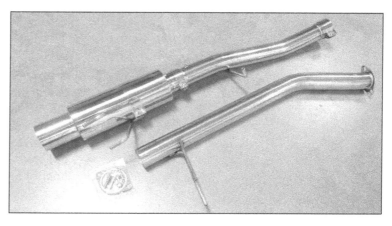

Installing a cat-back exhaust on a 240SX is extremely easy. The first section of pipe bolts up to the catalytic converter, and its lightweight hanger shaft slides right into the factory rubber exhaust mount. Be sure to install the ground strap from the heat shield on the chassis to one of the converter bolts and use the new gasket between the cat and this section of pipe.

The rear pipe slides into place over the first pipe, and the joint is secured with a large band clamp. All three of the hangers that supported this section lined up perfectly with the 240's factory rubber mounts. To complete the installation, make sure both clamps are snug and wipe the exhaust down to keep your fingerprints or other grease from staining the pipes.

The new Bullet exhaust hangs perfectly and it looks sick. And best of all, I won't have to change this exhaust system out no matter how much power I try to get out of my SR down the road.

HEATING AND COOLING SYSTEM

Remember those hoses I rerouted at the back of the engine? This is where that pays off. Even though they're now going in the right direction, you still have to connect the 3/4-inch hoses on the SR to the 5/8-inch heater-core fittings on the 240. With that in mind, I set aside a couple of leftover bent hose sections and picked up some 5/8ths hose with a right angle bend and a pair of 5/8-to-3/4-inch adapters. I had to go to two auto parts stores to get them, and both of the people I talked to looked at me funny when I told them what I wanted. They both told me they didn't have any—but they both did, so be persistent.

I made this setup with those 3/4-inch bent hoses, some hose clamps, a 30-degree fitting from the SR20DET, a 5/8-inch right-angle hose section from the KA, and one of those 5/8-to-3/4-inch adapters. Believe it or not, it fits perfectly between the lower heater core fitting and the fitting in the center of the SR intake manifold. Of course, all those joints are prone to leaks, but it will work in a pinch. I kept this one as a spare.

This is ultimately what I wound up with. That 5/8-inch right-angle hose only had to be cut down slightly and then joined to the 3/4-inch SR hose with an adapter. Notice that on this side of the hose clamp, I installed an insulated C-clamp to keep the hose from moving around. Just below that, instead of the previously pictured unit, I went with a single 5/8-inch hose off the KA. It was in good enough condition to reuse, but broken-in enough to slide over the larger, 3/4-inch fitting that you can't see under the SR intake. I also installed a new vacuum line between the engine and master cylinder.

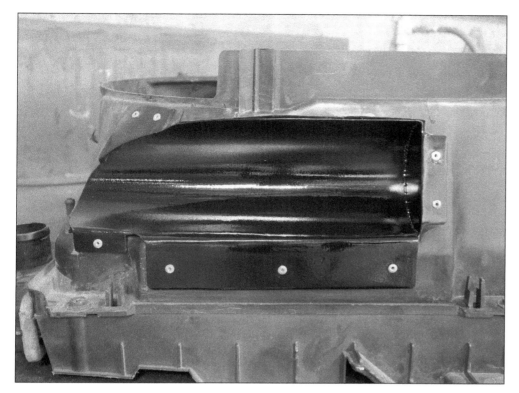

When I dropped the radiator and fan shroud in for the first time, I realized that the AC dryer was in the way. Because I wanted to keep the AC (remember, this car will be driven in Arizona) I cut out a section of the fan shroud, to accommodate the dryer. Of course, I felt it wasn't a good idea to leave such a large, gaping hole in the side of the fan shroud considering drift cars are already at a disadvantage where cooling is concerned. I made a sheetmetal patch, painted the whole thing black, and riveted it to the plastic shroud. You could also make the same thing out of fiberglass, ABS plastic, or PVC pipe—as long as it doesn't hit the fan, you're good. I also sealed the joints with black RTV silicone for good measure.

With the right clearance, the fan and shroud should drop right into place. I am using the stock fan, shroud, and obviously the stock clutch fan. I went with these due to the budget, and because I got a clean set with the front clip. Ideally I will upgrade the radiator to a Koyo or similar aftermarket unit designed for a 240 with an SR20DET swap (radiators meant for the stock KA24DE, stock or aftermarket, won't work because the outlets are on opposite sides).

With the radiator in place, install the intercooler piping just as it came off of the SR front clip. You may want to hook up the 240's power steering pump before you install the pipes from the intercooler to the turbo. Fortunately for me, this car was originally equipped with the KA24DE, which means the power steering is compatible with the SR and both hoses bolted right up to its pump. Below that, you can install either the KA or SR A/C compressor (I used the one from the KA). To use the SR compressor, which would be ideal, you need the hose fitting from the clip that will fit it—and this was the one part I gave away before I knew I needed it. I installed the KA compressor, which obviously worked with the A/C fittings, but I had trouble mounting it to the SR bracket—the KA bracket won't fit on the SR block. The bolt in the center of the SR bracket had to be removed so the compressor would sit flat, and even then only the two front bolts would line up. This appears to be enough to hold the compressor securely, but I will probably fabricate a bracket for a third bolt hole later down the line. This was also the best time to run a vacuum line from the fitting on the intake pipe (just above the power steering pulley, next to the green tape on the water outlet), which runs down to the factor blow-off valve.

With all that squared away, you can install the rest of the intake pipes between the turbo and intercooler, and the air intake. I decided to stick with the factory air box—a decision that will certainly raise a few eyebrows. Why not an aftermarket, open element intake? Because they are hard to find for the SR20DET and when you can find them, they're expensive. I have no faith in the $19.99, no-name pieces offered on the Internet. Plus, I can install one at any time since it's easy to get to. Until that time, I installed a fresh K&N filter that will not only flow freely, but also filter exceptionally.

WIRING

This brings me to everyone's favorite part of the job: wiring! Most people are terrified by the mere thought of cutting into a factory wiring harness, which makes this by far the most dreaded part of the SR20DET swap. At first, even I was a little intimidated by the thought of blending the KA and SR harnesses together and even considered one of the many services available to do it for me. In the end I decided to do it myself and found it was actually pretty easy. All you have to do is swap a few Molex plugs from one harness to the other and lengthen a few wires. If you're not afraid of a soldering iron, then you can do this for yourself.

The wiring all starts in the passenger's kick panel where the KA ECU is located. Unbolt it and unplug the large connecter, which is also secured with a bolt. Unplug the Molex plug just up from the ECU (notice the wire loom extending from the top of the ECU connecter up into the dash) and another up behind the climate-control fan motor just off the main harness. Loosen the bolt just behind the ECU on the white tab that holds the climate control fan motor and the wiring harness tab in place.

Under the hood, remove the large rubber grommet from the firewall and then carefully pull the KA harness through into the engine bay. At this point, my old KA had long been removed so the other end of the wiring harness was just lying in the engine bay, with the SR20DET already in place. Wiring companies typically spread the SR harness out on a large board marked with all the modifications they need to make, which helps guide the technician making the modifications. These boards tell them what Molex plug goes where and how long to make each of the wires that need to be extended. If you do it yourself, you can use the engine bay as your guide.

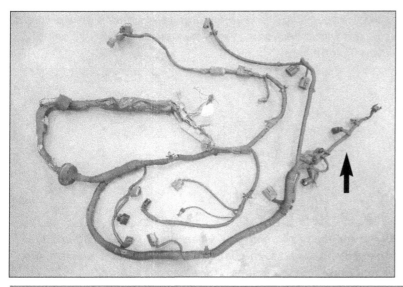

The SR20DET harness is easily identified by the rigid sections of wiring that connect to the fuel injectors and that run across the front of the engine to the mass airflow sensor (both located on the right side of this image). To make this harness work with the 240, you only have to change out two Molex plugs, make one adapter, and lengthen a couple of wires so that their respective Molex plugs reach to the other side of the engine bay—it's really not that bad. On the downside, this harness was slightly hacked up. You may have noticed the loose wires and duct tape by the main ECU connecter. I had to repair this damage and go over the entire harness in search of more damage—inspect your wiring prior to installation.

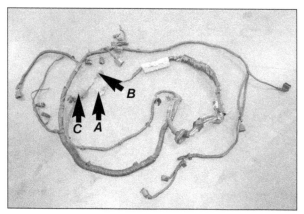

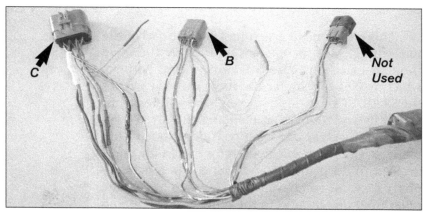

This is the KA harness I just removed. You'll need to harvest three of its Molex plugs to swap into the SR20DET harness: the tan plug (A) just off the end of the large ECU connecter and the brown (B) and grey (C) plugs just next to it in the photo. The big reason this harness isn't typically used is that the SR has a distributorless coil pack ignition, as opposed to the KA's traditional coil and distributor setup. The best wiring info can be found at www.srswap.com under SR Install FAQ. If you need to know where each wire from your ECU goes, go to the Nissan Silvia page at www.sr20det.nismo.org and click on SR Tech. You can also find an S13 Silvia wiring diagram on the Jim Wolf technology website at www.jimwolftechnology.com. It is all in Japanese, but if you can read a wiring diagram, the symbols will make sense. I found this useful for tracking down electrical problems.

The biggest job on the wiring harness was to swap the large grey (C) and smaller brown (B) Molex plugs from the KA engine harness onto the SR engine harness you see here. Simply cut the two Molex plugs off of the KA harness, but be sure to leave a sufficient length of wire to work with. There are three Molex plugs on the SR harness in this location, including the small black Molex with the blue and black wires (C), which will not be used. I felt there was no reason to remove it, so I just taped it to the harness. Remove the other two plugs from the SR harness, as they don't work with the U.S. 240SX. The plugs from the KA engine harness that will be used in their place are really easy to wire up. Just match color to color (plugs and wires), solder the harness wires to the Molex plug wires, and then cover them with heat shrink tubing. The one exception is the heavy-gauge black/red and blue/red wires on the SR harness side that were both attached to the one black/red wire on the KA Molex plug (that is the connection with the white heat shrink). Note that the orange and pink wires were not used and capped. You should also know that all the wires I attached to these KA plugs did not come directly from the plug they replaced on the SR harness. The green/yellow wire that was originally connected to the large grey plug on SR harness was wired to the smaller brown plug that came from the KA harness. The blue/green wire was just the opposite; it came from the smaller brown plug on the SR and was attached to the larger grey plug from the KA. You won't have to worry about this, however, as long as you match up the colors like I said. The wiring section on the www.srswap.com SR Install FAQ page is very helpful here.

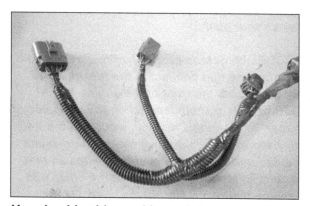

You should solder and heat shrink every wire you cut on this job because that makes a durable connection that will last over time, even in the engine bay. Of course I still covered my wires with split loom and electrical tape, too. It no only protects the wires from damage, but looks good as well.

Once in the car, the brown and grey Molex plugs simply plug into the KA car harness right next to the battery. After this shot was taken, they were tucked down into the fender where they came from.

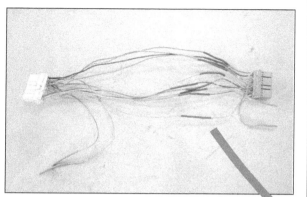

Because I had the SR front clip, I also had the complete car wiring harness. This is a harness that would not otherwise be needed, and is not the engine harness you need to get when you purchase just an engine. Rather than cut into the SR engine harness, or the KA car harness, to make these connections, I decided to cut the plug off the KA engine harness (A) where I got the other Molex plugs from (C and B), and the white harness off the SR car harness. This gave me the Molex plugs I needed to make an adaptor. All the wires lined up color to color except for the few that were not used and capped in blue. If you don't have access to this white plug, you can cut the other white plug off the SR car harness at the ECU plug and hard-wire the tan plug from the KA in its place. Make sure to give it some extra slack so that it will reach its plug on the car harness up in the KA's dash.

Just as the KA harness came out of the car, the SR harness needs to be fished in through the large hole in the firewall and its grommet installed. Mount the ECU that came with the front clip in the same location as the KA ECU you removed. The bolt holes don't line up, but this unit is easy enough to secure to the sheetmetal. Remember that it came from the other side of the car, so you'll want to orient it and the wiring harness so they fit neatly behind the plastic kick panel cover—and don't forget to plug in the Molex up behind the climate-control fan motor. Install the large blue ECU connecter and make sure it is pressed all the way in without damaging any of the pins. Finally, this is where I installed the adaptor from the previous photo.

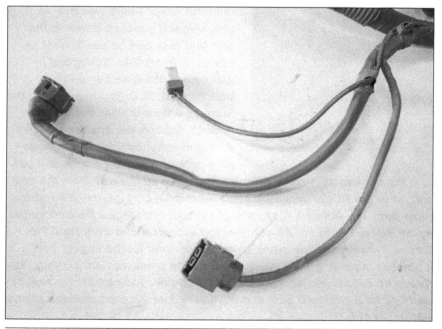

So far so good, right? Now for the easy part—the only thing left is to lengthen these connections. What I have here is the power steering plug (bottom), MAF plug (middle), and the A/C plug (top). You don't need to extend the A/C wire, as you should use the A/C wire from the KA car harness that is already over by the A/C compressor—but I extended this one before I realized that. The MAF uses a two-conductor shielded wire, which is just two regular insulated wires surrounded by loose wire strands and then covered in insulation. You should use shielded wire to lengthen these two leads. You can get it from the KA harness or a high-end electronics supply store. The loose wires used for shielding, on the section that is added, should be soldered to the loose wires on the harness and Molex plug at each end, just as if it were a third wire.

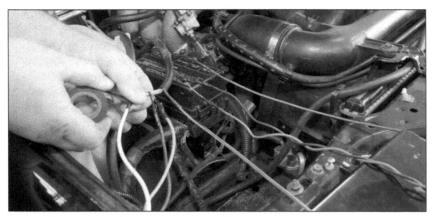

Now it's time to relocate the MAF and A/C plugs to the other side of the car. Just cut them off and solder new wire to their leads at the harness on the passenger side of the engine bay. Cover these wires in split loom and run them along-side the car harness, past the two Molex plugs I wired in next to the battery, and out through the inner fender. From there, run the wire through the core support just past the pop-up headlight and across the front of the car. Secure the wire loom along the way with zip-ties and make sure it won't interfere with any moving parts or come into contact with anything hot. Once on the driver side of the car, fish the wire loom through the core support near the charcoal canister and then cut the various wires to length.

The final task is to solder the respective ends back onto their lengthened wires. The insulation from both ends of each connection to be soldered should be stripped back about 1/4 inch and then the wires soldered together. Melt some heat shrink over the connections, and then cover everything with split loom and electrical tape. Plug them into their respective locations, and you're good.

As important as it is, I couldn't find a picture of the igniter, or where it went, anywhere on the Internet until I looked it up in eBay and found several for sale. Your car will not run without this piece, and neither did mine. In the JDM front clip, it was mounted to the driver side (left) on the strut tower (mine was not, as it was shipped separately due to the fact that they can be easily "lost in transit."). In my 240, it plugged in just behind the fuse box on the passenger side (right) near where the harness enters the car through the firewall. Igniters are easily damaged and somewhat difficult to diagnose as a problem, which I also found out.

Even once I installed the igniter into the SR harness, the car wouldn't start. After tracing wires all the way from the coil packs back to this spot and then from the other end on to the ECU, I was sure I had received a bad igniter—it happens. This is where buying your SR from a reputable source pays off. Autolink took care of me and exchanged the bad igniter for a good one. Once I plugged in the new unit, my car started right up. All of my wiring modifications were right the first time. Of course, before I attempted to start the car, I unplugged the crank angle sensor and let the engine turn over several times to get the oil flowing through it before I actually fired it up. Be sure the oil pressure light on your gauge cluster works and that you have sufficient pressure before you actually start your engine. You can also manually prime the oil pump. You should also drain your gas tank, fill it with new gas, and have your fuel injectors cleaned before you start your car. My new SR20DET didn't run right until I did.

FINISHED PRODUCT

That is pretty much what it takes to swap an SR20DET into a 240SX, and this is what the finished product should look like. The process is challenging, fun, and rewarding. I am not mechanic, but I found this swap to be simple enough that anyone with the right tools, some experience with cars, and the desire to do the job can easily do what I did here. I'm not saying this is for everyone, however. This chapter may serve as a guide for you to perform the swap yourself, or simply as reference material you can use in conjunction with a mechanic who will do the job for you. It may even make you think twice about keeping that KA. If you do the swap yourself, keep an open mind and do whatever research is necessary to resolve any problems that crop up. Good luck, and good drifting!

SOURCE GUIDE

240SX Motoring
(203) 783-1422
www.240sxmotoring.com

240SX.ORG
www.240sx.org

AEM
(310) 484-2322
www.aempower.com

Advanced Clutch
Technology (ACT)
(661) 940-7555
www.advancedclutch.com

B&M Racing &
Performance Products
(818)-882-6422
www.bmracing.com

Bob Bondurant
School of High
Performance Driving
(800) 842-RACE
www.bondurant.com

Bullet Exhaust
(562) 803-6122
www.jic-magic.com

Carfiche Dot Com
www.carfiche.com

Club4AG
www.club4AG.com

DC Sports
(310) 484-2322
www.dcsports.com

Denso
(888)-96-DENSO
www.densoiridium.com

DGTrials
www.dgtrials.com

Doug's Performance
Transmission
(480) 964-3832

Drift Acedemy
08707-60-70-44
www.driftacademy.co.uk

Drift Day
www.driftday.com

Drifting.Com
www.drifting.com

Drift Session
(808) 551-1164
www.driftsession.com

Drift Works by APC
(909) 898-9840
www.4apc.net

Energy Suspension
(949) 361-3935
www.energysuspension.com

Falken Tire Corporation
(800) 723-2553
www.falkentire.com

Fast Brake Enterprises
(602) 323-2110
www.fastbrakes.com

Fesler Productions
602-953-8944
www.feslerbuilt.com

Flex-A-Lite
(253) 922-2700
www.flex-a-lite.com

Formula D
www.formulad.com

G4 TV
www.g4tv.com

Goodyear
(330) 796-2121
www.goodyear.com

GReddy
(949) 341-9181
www.greddy.com

HASport Performance
(602) 470-0065
www.hasport.com

Heavy Throttle
Performance
(866) 4-SR-SWAP
(866-477-7927)
www.srswap.com

Initial D
www.initiald.com

Intense Motorsports
(480) 926-8797
www.intensepower.com

Jada Toys
www.jadatoys.com

JIC Magic
(562) 803-6122
www.jic-magic.com

Jim Wolf Technology, Inc.
(619) 442-0680
www.jimwolftechnology.com

Just Drift
www.justdrift.com

K&N Engineering, Inc.
(800) 858-3333
www.knfilter.com

Kaaz USA
(888) 522-KAAZ (5229)
www.kaazusa.com

Kelly Blue Book
www.kbb.com

Konig Motoring Accessories
(516) 822-5700
www.konigwheels.com

Koyo Cooling Systems, Inc.
888-557-KOYO (5696)
www.koyocooling.com

Napa Auto Parts
www.napaautoparts.com

Network Alignment
(602) 867-8061
www.networkalignment.com

Nismo Japan
www.nismo.co.jp/

Nismo USA
www.nissanusa.com

Nissan Silvia Page
www.sr20det.nismo.org

Phase2Motortrend
(909) 594-3619
www.phase2motortrend.com

The Progress Group
(714) 575-1193
www.progressauto.com

Show Off Cafe
www.showoffcafe.com

Speed Secrets
(877) 773-3310
www.speed-secrets.com

SPW Industries, Inc.
(909) 923-7500
www.spwindustries.com

TOKYOPOP
www.tokyopop.com

Toyota Salvage
(And Nissan)
(877) 807-4314
www.toyotasalvage.com

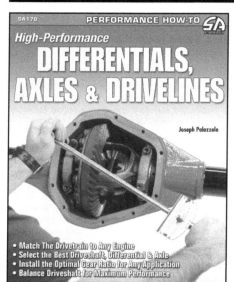
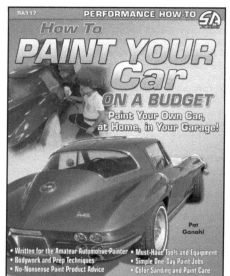

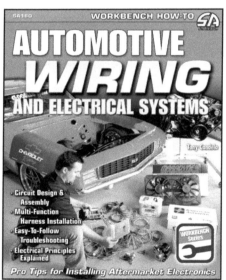

Milton Keynes UK
Ingram Content Group UK Ltd.
UKHW030418131223
434231UK00012B/578